The Greek-o-File
Volume 3

written & edited by
Sylvia & Terry Cook

The **Greek-o-File Volume** 3 published in Great Britain by Greek-o-File Ltd 2004
Copyright © Greek-o-File™ October 2004

ISBN 0-9543593-2-1

The **Greek-o-File Volume** 3 is the third compendium of new articles and anecdotes in paperback format written by Sylvia & Terry Cook and the many contributors acknowledged with their work. Photographs were supplied by authors of the relevant articles except where specified, illustrations are by Bibby Zinram (BZ), Diane Fryer and from free to use 'clipart'.

Edited and set: Sylvia Cook

Acknowledgements

The enthusiasm, feedback and contributions from subscribers to our first and second Greek-o-File books, published November 2002 and October 2003, and earlier quarterly magazines since 1998 have ensured a continuation of Greek-o-File in book format. We still depend on and thank those who continue to support us as direct subscribers and contributors. Our thanks especially to the contributors to this third volume and to Bibby Zinram for supplying illustrations to fill a few gaps.

We thank our advertisers and supporters, many since the early days of Greek-o-File, who have encouraged us as promoters of the 'real Greece' they believe in, as much as for commercial reasons.

Maps are an important part of travel notes and understanding the layout of a region. We are indebted to Efstathiadis and Road Editions for their kind permission to reproduce, adapt and use their maps.

We are also very grateful to the London Greek Embassy Press Office for their continuing support and to the AG Leventis Foundation for theirs.

Printed by: Cox & Wyman Ltd, Reading, Berkshire, UK

Greek-o-File Ltd, UK
Email: mail@greekofile.co.uk,
Website: www.greekofile.co.uk

Greek-o-File Volume 3 - Contents

Introduction

This third volume of The Greek-o-File contains more **new** entertaining articles, anecdotes and useful information for Grecophiles, in similar style to earlier editions. This is not a guide book, more a bumper size annual magazine - **a total Greek experience!**

Readers of earlier books have said how much they look forward to the next Greek-o-File compendium to bring a little Greek sunshine and *'filoxenia'* into their lives when they cannot be in their favourite country.

The articles written by fellow Grecophiles will inform and entertain you, whether you are an armchair traveller, a regular island hopper or someone who has a favourite part of Greece and friends you keep returning to. They may help you decide where to go next, or to recall happy moments and similar incidents that give you a warm feeling just thinking about them. Practical advice is offered for people who would like to spend more time in Greece and anecdotes of others' experiences may forewarn you of potential difficulties and the joys you could sample in the 'real' Greece of the Greeks.

2004 has been an exciting year for Greece - first as unexpected European Football Champions in Portugal, then as hosts of a very successful Olympic Games. Find out about the emotional and long lasting affect these events had on many.

When you have finished reading The Greek-o-File Volume 3, if you want to enjoy something of Greece back home, try some of the recipes, listen to the recommended Greek music and learn to tap along in time to the Greek rhythms, choose some of the reviewed books to immerse yourself further in the lives of the Greeks and those who have travelled to Greece, join fellow Grecophiles at a local Anglo Hellenic club or society, contact some of the advertisers to see what they have to offer - and maybe put pen to paper (or fingers to the keyboard) to share your own experiences of Greece with others for next year's Greek-o-File book.

We look forward to hearing from you.

Sylvia Cook

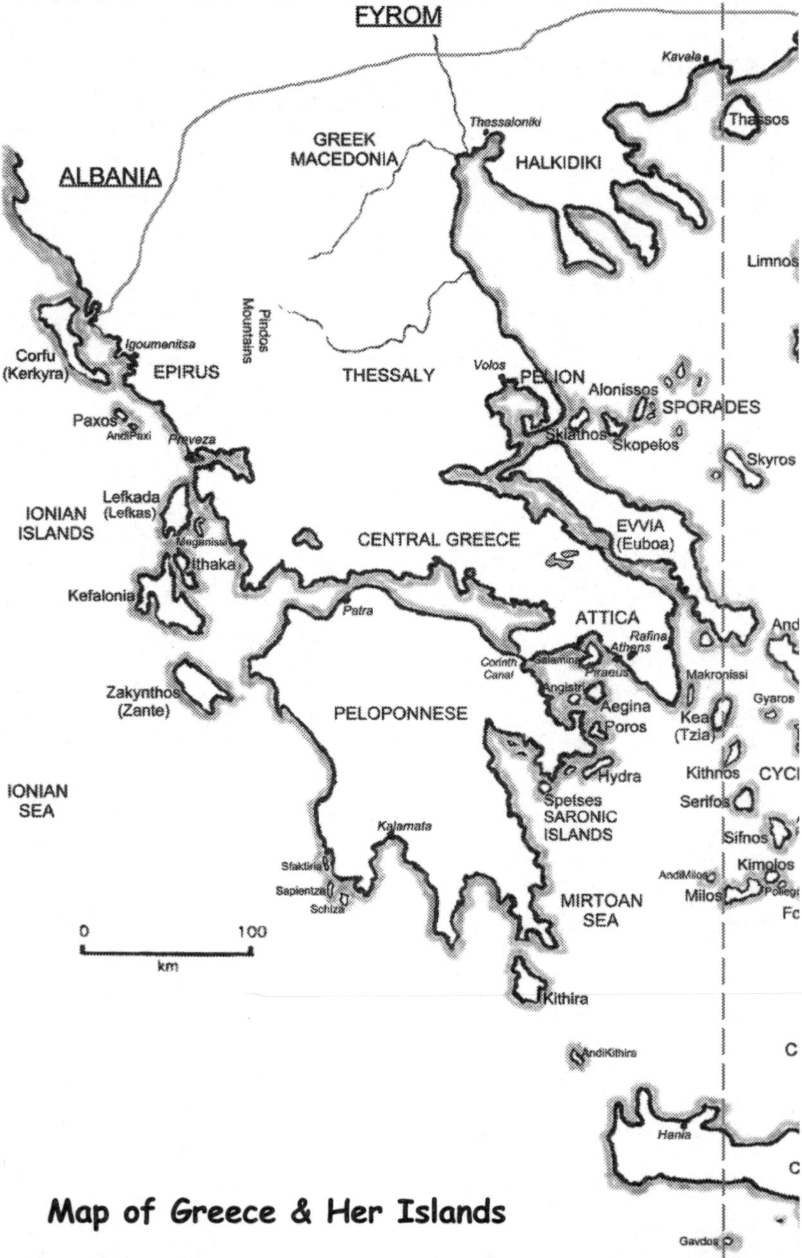

Map of Greece & Her Islands

Reference Map

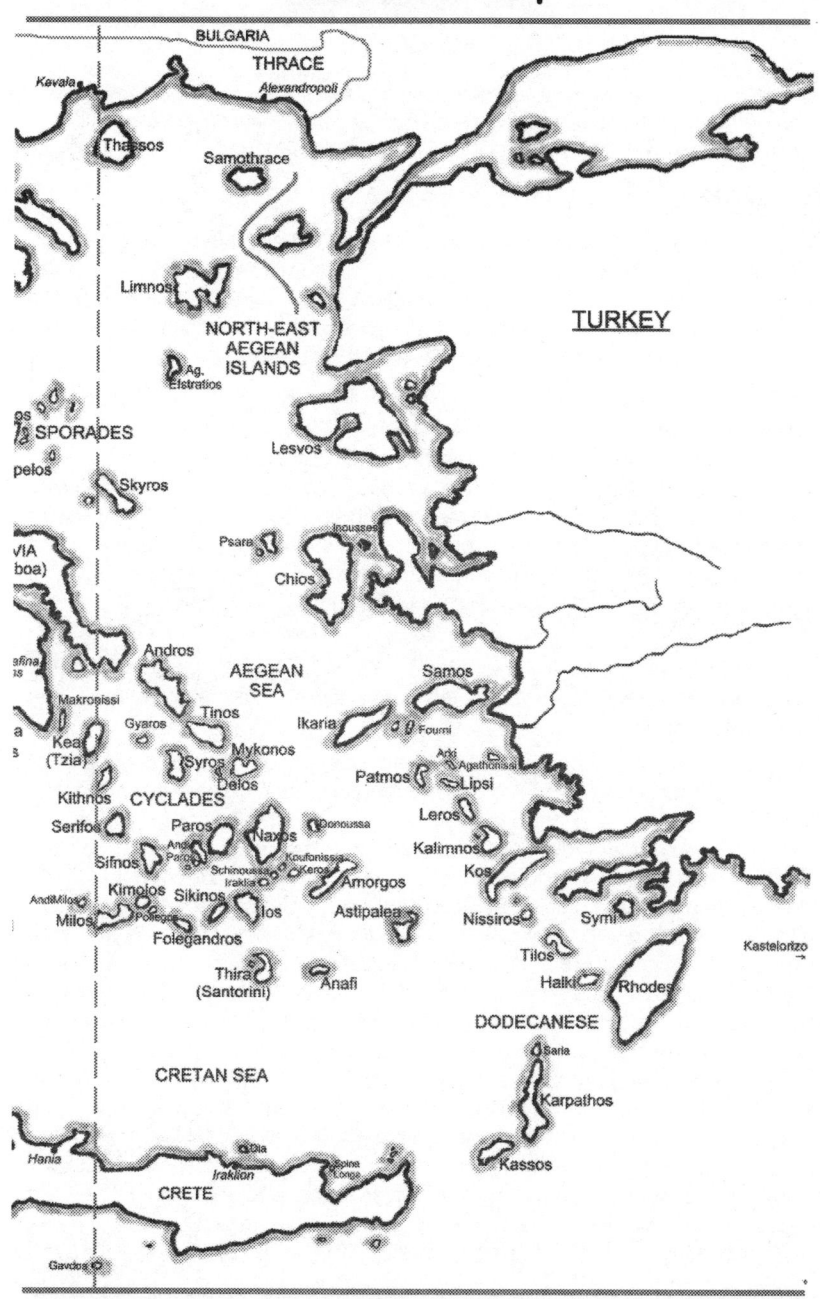

 # Life in Greece

'Life in Greece' will entertain and inform you with its wide range of articles and anecdotes from regular travellers to Greece and those who have made a new life there or have a second home in Greece. First Graeme Dakin tries to explain just what it is about Greece that makes him keep returning to the same country.

Cameos of Greece *by Graeme Dakin*

I have travelled to Greece many times for holidays in the last 20 years or so. I have visited a wide range of islands and mainland resorts and have never been disappointed. Friends and colleagues find this desire to return to the same country each year baffling and cannot understand why I have not been attracted to more *exotic* or *fashionable* destinations.

Just what is it that draws me back like a magnet to Greece each year ?

I recently spent a week on Crete in Almirida in the agricultural region of Apokoronas, close to Souda Bay, some 15 km east of Chania. This proved to be a wonderful holiday including so many small *cameos* which illustrate the charm (and frustrations) of Greece and its people and largely answer the above question. These are just some of the events and observations to illustrate my attraction to this wonderful country and its people.

Chaos Works - Arriving at Chania along with several other flights to find a number of baggage carousels disgorging luggage but with no indication of which carousel related to which flight. This is not unusual but illustrates what appears to be Greece's wholehearted devotion to their own version of *'the chaos theory'*.

This was further demonstrated at Chania bus station several days later. I had travelled on the early bus from Almirida to Chania to connect with a bus to Omalos at the top of the Samaria Gorge. On arrival at around 8.15, the temperature was already in the 80s and a throng of 100+ locals and tourists were huddled in the shade waiting for the mass departure of buses to all parts of the western half of the island at 8.30. At precisely 8.25 the loud-speaker crackled into life and the destinations for 15 or so buses and their bus number was announced in both Greek and English. This may have been reasonable if there were only 15 buses in the bus station and they were parked in numeric order, or perhaps grouped by regional destination. There were probably 60 buses in the bus station parked in random fashion and order resulting in locals and tourists running around frantically trying to find their bus under the burning early morning sun ....but it worked - and probably works every morning (and evening) of the year. At 8.30 precisely, all the buses made their way to the exit and dispersed to their different destinations without any obvious casualties being left behind. Whether everyone finished up where they intended to is another question. Initially, I found this infuriating but I simply had to laugh. There must be a better way of organising such things but it works in its own way, so who am I to criticise ?

Trust - Whilst walking through the small coastal town of Kalives, I noticed a small table outside a house displaying bags of oranges. A handwritten sign stated that the 2kg bags were for sale for 1 euro. No need to trouble the householder, you were trusted to place your payment in a tin on the same table. They were probably the tastiest and juiciest oranges I have ever tasted, and the freshest and best value.

Simple Tasty Food - On a mountain bike ride from Almirida to the only freshwater lake in Crete at Kournas, I eventually started on the downward slope towards my destination. In the village of Exopolis, I decided that I needed food and refreshment to bolster my energy. I stopped at Dimitris Taverna which at first glance appeared only to be inhabited by half a dozen sleeping cats. An elderly lady appeared at the door and ushered me into the shade of the building to a table overlooking the surrounding lush countryside and mountains. I asked for a beer and a Greek salad. This would be no problem she assured me and after serving my ice-cold Amstel busied herself preparing my Greek salad. I heard a lot of clanking of pots and pans in the kitchen area which puzzled me somewhat. Around half-an-hour later, I understood why. A huge Greek salad arrived including sliced, freshly cooked potatoes, accompanied by Cretan greens in olive oil and chunks of local bread. A simple but tasty meal that certainly filled the gap and more, all for less than €6.

Filoxenia - Whilst walking in the hills above Rethymnon, I arrived at the village of Chromonastiri in great need of refreshment after a particularly dusty, hot section of countryside. I searched, initially in vain, for a kafeneion or taverna where I could quench my thirst and eventually I stumbled on a

Cameos of Greece - 'Goat Rush Hour' on Kos back road

table outside what appeared to be a refreshment stop. On sitting down, a young boy aged only about 6 enquired in perfect English what would I like to drink. My cold beer appeared in a flash and after serving it, he enquired, again in immaculate English, where I was from. Whilst gulping the first mouthfuls of my beer, I noticed the boy's grandmother disappear across the road into a house. She returned with a large hunk of local bread and a correspondingly large block of local cheese and handed them to me. This was a welcome and unexpected snack. I felt really guilty when she would not accept more than one euro in payment. A good example of the legendary Greek filoxenia.

A Desire to Help - In Almirida, I asked for a spanakopita (spinach pie) at the bakery. The lady serving apologetically explained that she would not have any until the next day. On overhearing this, the delivery man rushed out to his van and conjured one up from nowhere! No doubt a delivery to a subsequent bakery was now one spanakopita short but he was just delighted to have helped me out.

Generosity - Most evenings I ate at a taverna in the village of Plaka, a short distance above Almirida. The taverna was dominated by 'mine host', a large, well built young lady who ran an efficient operation out front while her mother and remaining family slaved away in the kitchen. The food was excellent and was served in huge portions. This led to an ongoing discussion each evening when diners, on being asked why they had not eaten all of their food, explained that the food was superb but the portions were just too large. 'Mine host' was relieved to hear this but then insisted that the portions were not large just a normal size. This was debatable when individual Greek salads arrived in large basins and portions of moussaka resembled a house brick in size! After believing that you had successfully negotiated the food, fresh fruit (melon, apricots etc.) appeared accompanied by a bottle of raki to finish off the meal. This, of course, was free and certainly made the return walk (fortunately downhill) no problem at all, allowing me to reflect on the generosity of the Greek islanders, the beauty of the moonlit landscape and the incredible brightness of the thousands of stars in the night sky.

Endearing Sights - Looking for illustrations from my trips over the years, a few other cameos came to mind including sunbathing ducks in Stoupa, live turkeys wandering through a Corfu taverna, herds of goats on back roads, 'free range' pigs living in caves with magnificent views above Kefalos in Kos and this 'talking forest' in Zakynthos.

The overwhelming charm and generosity of the Greek people and their idiosyncrasies, the varied and dramatic landscapes, the marvellous climate and the chance to eat natural, delicious food *al fresco* provide everything that I need in a holiday.

I challenge anyone to go to the Greek Islands for a week's holiday and not return calmer and more able to put our manic, modern lives into a little more perspective.

Cameos of Greece (2) A Magical Land *by John Peverill*

Another answer to the same question arrived from John Peverill who said *"the poem says it all - the smells, taste, what we hear, see and feel. Greece becomes a part of the soul."*

Greece has a magic of simplicity,
No airs and graces, just vivacity,
True beauty in Spring with colours in swathes
A sea of new life in glorious waves.
Rustic old roads in avenues of pink
Look out on blue calm for mind drifts to think.
Orangy tinge as sun clambers from sleep
Shyness encouraged from covers to peep.
Peace swells from earth to the heavens above
Fathoms of calm float a raft of new love.
Unflustered life rises early to work
Abstaining the heat in shadows to lurk.
Blissfulness rests in the palm of her hand
Friendly welcome allures far from this land.

Cameos of Greece (3) Crowded Beaches *by Derek Robson*

The beach at Gerakas, Alonisos can get crowded at times!

Eco-Tourism, Managing the Change
by Paul Delahunt-Rimmer

Managing inevitable change has been one of the most difficult and challenging aspects of business since that earliest of tourists, Noah, set about releasing his passengers into a new land. Had this land been one of the Greek islands well known to the tourists of today he would have thought them to be beautiful and idyllic. Even forty years ago the shores and villages of the likes of Rhodes and Ios were peaceful, tranquil places to visit. As a visitor you could sit on the harbour front drinking Greek coffee and struggle to understand the shop signs and local people who were keen to hear of your life 'abroad'. You would enjoy walking along the old donkey paths and be greeted by the farmers and welcomed into their houses for fresh baked bread and olives from their groves. You had probably spent days on a ship to get there but it was worth it to see these sights and experience a different way of life.

Forty years on, vast tracts of these islands have been ruined; they are now just tourist resorts in the sun. The fields are bare and the fishing fleets practically non existent as the families turn to servicing the demand of the tourists. No longer can you experience the 'real Greece' on these islands. I believe that it is not the tourists that are to blame but the planners, developers, councils and local governments. The local people, in their naivety, consider that greater resources will generate greater income.

Short of a nuclear explosion there can be nothing more damaging to remote locations such as the Greek islands than sudden unplanned tourism development. The consequences to the physical environment may well destroy the very resource that attracted the tourist's attention in the first place. The rivers and coastlines become contaminated. The sea breeze carrying the aroma of herbs and flowers becomes polluted with exhaust emissions and aircraft fumes. The sounds of donkeys braying and the waves breaking on the beach are drowned out by beach discos and concrete mixers. Bright street lights block out the deep blue star sparkling Mediterranean night sky. There is congestion at the ports and in the villages that looks more like London a week before Christmas than a remote Greek island. Road and hotel building causes soil erosion, damages vegetation and wildlife and destroys natural and ancient man-made features.

These islands have seen many changes in the last 50 years. This change however has to be carefully planned, controlled, monitored and managed. Sadly, in the majority of cases it is not. They are ruining the very resources they are working to preserve and will not realise until it is too late. The more remote islands, particularly those without airports, have a very short tourist

season, some as little as six weeks. The way forward is not to increase capacity for this short period but to put strategies in place to lengthen the season and manage this growth through eco-tourism.

The three aspects of tourist capacity that should be considered are the *Physical*, the *Environmental* and the *Ecological* capacities (Holloway 1985; Lavery 1987). The physical capacity should be limited to control the other two. The environmental capacity is the maximum number of tourists an area can accommodate without a decline in the general perceived attraction of that area. Ecological capacity is the maximum number of visitors an area can take before ecological decline takes place. In the latter case taking appropriate measures can increase overall numbers.

The island of Amorgos where we live is, like many others, at its tourist optimum. It is outstandingly beautiful. A new road ensures better links between the few villages and there are just the right number of tavernas and pensions to give visitors a choice. Some of our footpaths through the mountains are now maintained making easier access to remote

Ormos, Aegiali

areas of beauty and interest. Conservation and the preservation of natural areas have emerged as important spill-over benefits of tourism. The protection of the very resources that visitors come to enjoy enhances and perpetuates tourism by maintaining its very foundation.

Marketing strategies and eco-tourism programmes should be developed to promote the environment and encourage increased tourism in the low season.

There are 3,000 islands of Greece of which only 170 are inhabited. A mere handful of these are genuinely unspoilt yet are still capable of supporting a reasonable and financially viable level of tourism. The aging world population means the trend is moving away from the noisy crowded tourist centres to these quieter resorts. With tourism comprising more than 20% of Greece's export income surely they must realise that protection, not exploitation, of their valuable resources is 'development'.

We couldn't agree more!

The Periptero *by Sylvia Cook*

In every city, every town, village and tourist resort, you cannot fail but notice the 'periptero' (περίπτερο), that small kiosk in the square, along the prom-enade or near a street corner, packed full of cigarettes, sweets and crisps for sale and usually with additional items on offer from fridges and drinks chiller cabinets, postcard and newspaper stands that surround the small wooden box. In many areas you will have several within sight of each other to choose from. The periptero is a fact of Greek life.

Sometimes you can barely detect the person sat inside between the wares which adorn the two sides and front of the small wooden box (always 1.9 square metres, I be-lieve) and hang from the wider roof which provides shade for customers and goods. But there is a small window through which you can request ciga-rettes, telephone cards, mobile phone (*kinito*) pay-as-you-go cards and more. Through this small hole you show the items taken from outer displays and pay for your goods, usually placing your money and taking change from a large ashtray like dish.

Cigarettes and tobacco are the main sales from these little boxes. One tobacco sales licence is granted for every 400 local inhabitants and most of these will be for periptera (plural) - more than 46,000 periptera in the whole of Greece. Even with the lower prices in Greece, a large proportion of the tobacco price is for tax, so these small businesses sell other items appropri-ate to their location - map books and guides, parking display tickets, bus tickets, stamps, bottles of chilled water and ice creams to cool the summer passer-by.

The licence for a periptero is traditionally granted to ex-servicemen wounded in action or to ex-policemen injured on duty - perhaps as a kind of war pension or work opportunity. In most cases they are rented out to a more able bodied person for a regular income, but you will occasionally come across a 'wounded' soldier inside. In key sites they can be very lucrative for the owner and/or the person renting the business.

I can't say that I would relish the thought of working long hours in such a confined space and winter cannot be a comfortable or pleasant time to sit in a drafty periptero box awaiting the occasional customer who has braved the elements to satisfy his or her tobacco craving or sweet tooth. The ones we see mostly have electric fires in the winter and a small television to help while away the hours, but it can be a long day. They are usually attended from early morning until late in the evening - whatever the weather.

The periptera of Greece provide more than a convenient sales outlet, they invariably provide a service too. If you are ever lost in a city or town, ask at the periptero and perhaps buy a map as well. If you need to understand parking locally, or know when the next bus runs, just ask at the nearest little kiosk and maybe buy your ticket at the same time.

In a land of many small businesses, there is something about a periptero that is quintessentially Greek.

DIY - Necessity or Pleasure *by Sylvia Cook*

Our story of rebuilding our Greek home in Eresos, Lesvos continues with rather less uncertainty or urgency since writing about the disaster, when our little village house burnt down, for Volume 1 and the trials and tribulations of organising rebuilding and dealing with authorities related in Volume 2.

Now it's all down to us.

Our village is one of those that lost a massive percentage of people in the 1950s when opportunities abroad encouraged many to emigrate to Australia, America, Africa and other parts of the world. When Terry first bought Spiti Cook (in his lawyer's name) 15 years ago there were many dilapidated empty houses around the village. Since that time purchasing property in border territory is no longer an issue for other EU residents so families have been selling off their unused assets and with their increased incomes have been renovating their own houses and building new homes. The builders, carpenters, electricians and plumbers are kept very busy and it is sometimes impossible to find someone **when** you want them to do a job for you.

The lack of sufficient tradesmen, coupled with the nature of many Greeks who are impossible to tie down to appointments on a specific day, let alone a specific time, AND the probability that you will not get exactly what you thought you asked for, make DIY a preferable option for many house owners, for all but the most skilled tasks.

We had decorated the old house several times, tiled the new bathroom, patched up holes with Polyfilla (or equivalents from UK), learnt to use locally available *'gypsos'* (like plaster of paris) for other projects, fixed cupboards, made small tables and brought friends and family out to help replace the old kitchen roof and build a staircase. These projects were completed while we holidayed with the restriction of minimal holiday allowances from employers - hence there was always something to do over the years.

Now we have given up regular incomes we can spend longer periods in Greece, but obviously have less cash available to pay others. DIY wherever possible is a necessity for us, but we have also enjoyed making things for our own house and learning new skills. It is very satisfying and often less frustrating than trying to get others to do work for you when it suits you.

We've used professionals for major essential works, but Terry's carpentry has moved up a level and I am very impressed with the new bed he made on our December trip - so much more comfortable than the mattress on the floor we started with when we moved in last summer.

Like most tasks here, the design evolved. With only a small bedroom, we had thought we could build our new bed to sit above a ledge claiming an

extra 15cm room width. The frame was built, slats placed, then the thick mattress put on top. I was busy painting when Terry came to ask for my approval before positioning the 'headboard' - two covered pillow cushions hanging from a pole on the wall. We decided to sleep on it for one night, but it was fairly obvious that the bed was too high. We were close to the ceiling

when we sat up to drink our morning coffee! Next day he sawed a good length off and refinished each leg, still leaving just enough space for some storage boxes to slide underneath. The sawn off legs later made good short legs for one of our couches/ guest beds upstairs.

If we had realised that we could not raise our bed above the ledge we may have bought one, but Terry's bed is not only more robust it was also cheaper and doesn't have one of the annoying design features of our previous Greek wooden slatted bed lost in the fire. It used to annoy me every time I struggled to tuck the sheets in as the mattress sat exactly within a deep rectangle. I was forever grazing my knuckles, or breaking nails. The new bed has a flat area for the mattress and I'm promised a low raised edge around the corners to stop the mattress sliding before I get round to varnishing it.

Getting the right materials is often a problem. Our island now has more available in local hardware shops and better supply shops in the centre of the island (Kalloni, over 1 hour away) but nothing like the choice in DIY chain stores in the UK, nor special offers and competitive sales prices. Local carpenters will supply and cut wood to size, but at an extra cost. The main wood store in Kalloni now supplies to the general public as well as trade buyers. Although prices are quite good, it can be difficult to get exactly what you want. The dimensions offered are not those we are used to and they do not cut to size. With all the work we needed doing we invested in a number of appropriate power tools to replace and improve on those lost in the fire.

Last summer we had the 'grekovan' our ex-minibus motorhome, so we brought a lot of things with us where UK prices made it worthwhile. During that trip there was little we could not collect for ourselves from the Kalloni wood shop. In December, having flown here, we had a small hire car for a few weeks then no transport. They do deliver, but only when they have enough to make it worthwhile AND if the weather is dry. It is not possible to stay in the house every day on the off-chance that a delivery will arrive, but, unusually, we did get a call a week after ordering a 4 metre beam (to divide our open plan room with a rail and curtain), to say it would be with us the next day before 10 am. It was our last day with the hire car and we planned another trip to Kalloni for Christmas supplies and more wood. We waited until 11 am, but finally asked at the local shop if they would take delivery. Getting to the wood shop an hour and a half later we were told the lorry had not gone because of the rain. The beam eventually turned up after Christmas.

Pre-Christmas we ordered a sheet of MDF 'the same as last time' (they have our purchase history on their database) but that did not arrive with the beam. No phone calls this time, but it eventually turned up 10 days later - the *only* day we were out with friends. We got back to find a large 2 x 3m board propped against our outside wall. It was twice as thick as the one we'd had before, but we'd paid for it and thought it would make a more sturdy structure. It would have been just too difficult and time consuming to have it collected and the correct one delivered - and Terry was itching to start the new project.

It was no mean feat, man (and woman)-handling it over the top of our gate and into the courtyard. A girlfriend was with us and little Maria from 2 doors down (5 foot maximum and very slight) was passing and gallantly helped. There was no way we would get it inside the house in one piece (rain was expected) so we made some hasty measurements and plans for the bench seat and Terry got out his power saw to cut it into 3 pieces.

The bench is completed now and another success story, though not quite as originally planned! It certainly won't be moving from its place in our sitting room very much. Terry and I struggled to lift it from the other end of the room where he had constructed it with two of the heavy board pieces on a framework of wood, with the front and

sides made from leftover pieces of floorboard wood - a seriously robust piece of furniture! With one mattress on top and another cut down and re-upholstered for the back, leaning against a frame, it is very comfortable. It will double as a guest-bed and storage for bedding and is also a good height for sitting at our table when we have winter dinner guests (in the summer we usually eat outside). It looks quite traditional too with its stripey cream and beige 'throw' and cushions along the back.

I must confess to being mainly on painting, varnishing and tiling du-ties, and holding large pieces of wood while Terry saws them, or 'general labourer' and occasional cement mixer. I'm not good at wielding saws, planes and screw-drivers, but I enjoy being involved in the planning (and often re-plan-ning) stages. Occasionally we have a clash of understanding, but the end result is usually strong and  'rustic,' which fortunately we both like for our Greek village home.

A new friend we've made, who has a holiday home here, is much stronger and practical - just as well as her German husband does not get involved with her construction projects. She has built wardrobes, made a bed-settee and more, and being Greek she knows how to ask for what she wants from local tradesmen in no uncertain terms! And yet, she says she does not always get a good job done in the way she wants it, so she may as well 'do it herself' as well as she can. At least she knows what is acceptable to her and what is not. Her projects all look very professional to us.

Another couple who retired here a number of years ago had an old cottage half rebuilt and have got into DIY out of necessity. Although built as a strong stone house, the staircase put in by a third party subcontract 'carpenter' was really unacceptable. After a few wide steps to a platform it became a steep ladder with very close steps that necessitated walking backwards to get down. They put up with it for a few years, often cursing the so-called 'carpenter' as they edged down at night to go to the bathroom. The building project had taken longer than expected, eating into their funds while they rented elsewhere, and the total cost was more than quoted and anticipated, as is often the case. Gradually they have improved and added to the house, mostly themselves - a bench seat where a rock face cut into the house, flyscreens at windows, canopies over windows and doors. Finally having had several expensive quotes for replacing the stairs (which they could ill-afford from pension income) and with advice from a couple of people, they went ahead and made their own staircase for a fraction of the cost. The result - an easy to climb and descend, attractive staircase that fits into a slightly smaller overall area AND they have a lot more confidence now to tackle more major projects.

We had a few more major projects too - like the storage platform above the office end of our open plan room (for boxes, suitcases, clothes, spare books, etc) which was successfully completed in the summer along with painting and varnishing walls and ceilings. Plans for the sunshine water heater were brought forward as we cleared out the rat-visited end of the apothiki to construct a new roof and seal it from uninvited visitors. Of course we needed to buy the heater to know how best to support it on the roof, so it was fitted between snow and storms in January, working with local help for roofing, lifting, plumbing and thinking on this more complex project. On our return in spring we were hugely impressed by our 'free hot water' in the summer months, but did wire up the electrics for winter use.

Working on our own house and making things for it has been immensely satisfying as well as cheaper. We also feel that our personal efforts have earned us the respect of many locally. Often even the poorest people here would not dream of making things for themselves, or even painting walls.

At the end of 1999 we wrote about DIY 'Greek Style' for our former quarterly magazine. Not much has changed since then on our island, but practice does make perfect (or a little closer to it) and as long as you are reasonably able-bodied you may find a little unaccustomed manual labour benefits your health as well as your pocket. Terry actually lost weight working on the house in Greece last summer.

So, if you have a Greek home and a basic tool kit, you just need an abundance of **Patience** and **Flexibility** to **Do It Yourself**. Go on! You might just find that what seems a chore in Britain is enjoyable in a Greek village. Somehow everything in Greece is more fun.

Lessons from Our Samos Sojourn *by Anne Richardson*

If DIY and home ownership does not appeal to you, these lessons from Anne and her husband Ron on their first long trip to Greece may suggest an alternative and alert you to some potential problems through their experience of living in Greece.

Having travelled all over Greece (42 different locations, islands and mainland, when we stopped counting), we finally found Samos. We then visited Samos 18 times before we decided to retire early, take the plunge and try a longer slice of island life. On our last holiday we found, through word of mouth, a house to rent for a year. We returned to England, made systematic lists of requirements, found a carrier and shipped a huge box of essential 'goodies' out to our new home.

I left work on 31st March and we flew to Samos on 1st April!

Psili Ammos, near to our Votsalakia home

Naturally, with this being Greece, the box of essentials did not arrive until three weeks after we did. The box had been on the island since the agreed delivery date but the lorry expected to deliver it to our home was at the 'wrong' port, disruption due to a storm! To add insult to injury, the lorry driver who delivered the box then requested a further €50 for the 'home delivery'. My husband refused to pay this. Our paperwork clearly showed we had already paid the rate required for delivery to our address. Our Greek friend who supervised the delivery warned us that they all try it on! **Lesson 1: Don't trust everyone.**

Life did not begin as planned. We suffered torrential rainstorms, much to the amusement of friends and family in England who delighted in telling us of the unseasonable Mediterranean weather they were enjoying at home. **Lesson 2: Greek weather is no longer predictable.**

The brand new house we had rented leaked copiously through the balcony doors, down the inside walls, onto the living room floor. The walls became porous as they had not yet been painted on the outside, and everywhere felt very damp. The bathroom window frame also leaked and this caused floods over the entire surface of the large bathroom floor. (Unpleasant to walk on at night, in fabric slippers, when one needed to visit the loo!) When the leak problems were pointed out to our landlady, (she speaks virtually no English, and our Greek at that time was VERY basic), she intimated that all Greek houses leak. Apparently everyone has to put up with leaking walls, windows etc. because the builders do not make houses to cope with the unusual weather being experienced nowadays! However, she did promise that her husband would seal the leaks with silicone once the drier weather arrived and that the walls would be painted in May. The landlady later revised the timetable for painting until October, but by the time we left the house in December neither the paint nor the silicone had materialised.

Lesson 3: Do not believe Greek promises.

Pluses from the early weeks included: delight in the sheer number and variety of wild flowers carpeting every available piece of earth; a huge number of migratory birds spotted around our house and garden (67 different species properly identified and many others that we failed to identify due to our in-expertise); a warm welcome from the locals; peace and quiet to enjoy the

sights and sounds before the tourists arrived; adoption of us by 'Wheezer Billy' (an asthmatic tomcat) and his two 'wives'; a day trip to try to spot the Monk Seals breeding at a cove further up the coast. (We failed to find them but did discover previously unexplored areas of the island).

Minuses included: the interminable day and night impregnation of the local female cats by every male tomcat in the olive tree just under our bedroom window, involving fights and howling for nearly four weeks; the daily arrival of more and more feral cats each with begging bowl and a procession of dependent relatives; frustration at trying to 'suss out' the Greek way of doing things so that you achieve your objectives; inability to obtain a telephone line (again due to false promises by the landlady); news from home of the loss of our beloved, elderly English cat who had absconded from her 'foster home'.

However, we quickly settled in, and concentrated on the production of our 'little book of walks'. We had mapped out the area around Kambos (Votsalakia) on our previous trips and I had spent hours writing the walk instructions and drawing the maps ready to produce the book for use by the first tourists of the season. This book proved to be a roaring success and we were inundated by requests for copies. *(Still available, regularly updated, contact us by email at ron@ronrichardson.wanadoo.co.uk).*

Early in May we were invaded, awoken at 4 am by the sound of a male voice shouting *"Hut, hut"*. Under our bedroom window we heard the clatter of

hooves and the swishing of vegetation; our garden had become the breakfast bar for dozens of goats. The shepherd was trying valiantly to round up

the errant beasts but they were more interested in grazing on our *horta* than heeding his instructions. As a result, we had to work out how best to clear up huge amounts of goats' *poo* from our driveway – Greece certainly provides learning opportunities of the most unexpected kind.

Early summer saw another unexpected visitor. An elderly lady appeared early one morning dragging bundles of weeds across our patio. She smiled and stashed her bundles at the end of our driveway. My husband offered her a cup of coffee. In pidgin Greek and sign language we ascertained that she was only fifty years old, had a herd of goats up the coast at Limnionas, but had exhausted her supply of goat fodder up there. She was collecting anything edible from anywhere not fenced in.

Lesson 4: If you don't have a fence, your land is their land.

Two weeks later she brought us some home-produced Feta and Mizithra cheeses, 18 eggs and a bunch of wild flowers as a 'thank you'! She then asked me for a dress because hers was worn out. I gave her an old sundress. She was delighted, saying she would wear it when she took her herd down to the beach - if you visit Limnionas, look out for her.

Lesson 5: Greeks can be immensely generous.

The most frustrating (terrifying?) event of the year for me was the discovery of a metre-long snake curled up in the corner of our upstairs lounge. It was impossible to identify quickly from the book of amphibians I had brought from England and we had to rely on our landlord to deal with it. He did - he scooped it up, threw it on the balcony and clubbed it to death with our sun umbrella pole. When we tried to ascertain whether it had been dangerous

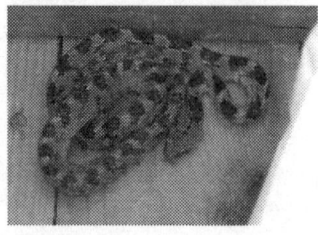

or not, the locals were divided. Some said *"very"*, others *"not so"*, but who should we believe? I finally managed to identify the snake by careful examination, after its demise. It was a cat snake, venomous, but unlikely to be dangerous to humans, due to its small jaws. But, everyone agreed that they had never heard of a snake managing to climb to a first floor room. We finally found out that snakes can, and do, climb trees. There was an olive tree overhanging our balcony and this was the only way it could have entered our house. Needless to say, the next day we sawed all overhanging branches down.

Lesson 6: Don't assume the locals know their own wildlife.

The sojourn was not entirely without medical problems. My husband was bitten by one of the many horseflies that delight in chasing humans. He reacted so badly that his leg and foot grew to double their normal size very quickly, whilst we were taking friends around the island in our hired car. He could not operate the car pedals effectively due to the swelling. Luckily we located a very proficient chemist who sold us medicine and cream which, after a four hour rest, relieved the symptoms sufficiently to enable him to drive us home. The pain and swelling did not completely go for over a week.

One morning I suffered the shock of finding most of my back molar tooth in pieces after I had eaten my breakfast. (I had dutifully visited my dentist in England just before we had left for Samos, hoping my teeth would be trouble-free until our return). With help from a Greek friend I found a dentist. As instructed I just walked into her office at about 1 pm. She spoke virtually no English. I had a Greek phrase book open at the appropriate page for 'Visiting the Dentist'. With sign language, pidgin Greek and pidgin English, we communicated. It took over an hour to repair the tooth; the equipment was reminiscent of that used in England in the 1950s, (low speed drill, HUGE hypodermic needle, etc.), no dental nurse, no frills, but the filling was a masterpiece of dental engineering, worth every penny of the €50 cost. (Incidentally, our insurance has a £50 excess so treatment was a private expense.)

Lesson 7: Minor healthcare is efficient and effective.

On a blisteringly hot September day we were enjoying the cooling effect of the air conditioning unit in our house, when Greek friends called and invited us to an instant 'treat'. We piled into their car and set off for the nearby village

of Ormos. Here we were amazed to be greeted by a parade of immaculate, classic and vintage cars. They were driven in convoy down the narrow village streets, parked on the scruffy harbour front, gleaming in the sun, whilst their proud owners lunched in the harbour-side tavernas. It was so incongruous. Who would ever have expected to see cars that would have

taken pride of place at Beaulieu Motor Museum, parked on waste ground, in a little Greek backwater village? An unexpected, free and magical treat.

Lesson 8: Expect the unexpected!

Do not assume your partner will react in the same way to the 'ex-pat' life as you do. I found the whole sojourn interesting and fascinating; my husband however found the lack of familiar faces and routines difficult. He became immensely bored with what he felt was 'the overly laid-back, nonspecific, point-lessness of day to day life'. He was surprised that he disliked the 'long holiday' feel and found time sometimes dragged without his beloved garden and sheds to potter in. During the tourist season we had little interaction with the Greeks who mostly worked from early morning until late at night in tourist related activities, so, unless we went to tavernas, we were very much on our own. I can honestly say that I was never bored or homesick. Obviously you miss family and friends but an occasional telephone chat, text messages and letters were enough for me. We had discussed this aspect before we left England, but the reality proved different and we had to rethink to try to solve the problem. We revised the division of household chores, planned specific weekly activities and shortened our planned stay.

Lesson 9: Be prepared for homesickness and communicate.

Finally, (and perhaps the most worrying) is the need to learn to regulate your intake of alcohol. Neither of us have ever been social drinkers. In England, we only drank wine with meals at weekends, accompanied by an occasional aperitif. Moving to Greece and embracing the culture involved drinking far more alcohol than we had ever been used to. It became the norm to sit with friends in a taverna over a beer at lunchtime. Late afternoon often involved a chat with Greek friends and ouzo would appear. With evening meals we usually had a glass, or two, three, or more of wine. Once we realised, we both made a concerted effort to limit our alcohol intake, but this caused consternation amongst Greek and non-Greek friends. Eventually we had to relate our abstinence to our (real) stomach conditions, (gall bladder and hiatus hernia) before we were able to socialise, acceptably, without alcohol! It seems the alcohol issue is problematical with others who have moved to Spain, Italy and Portugal too.

Lesson 10: Watch your alcohol consumption.

All in all it was an interesting year, perhaps different from our expectations but enjoyable nonetheless - so much so that we are doing it again, but moving to a leak-free apartment with a garden and a shed.

PS July 2004: Pleased to report that our change of residence on Samos resulted in an absolutely idyllic three month visit to Samos this spring. We are so very happy now in our new accommodation and everything else has just improved enormously as a result. It just goes to show how important finding the right house is - another salutary lesson for anyone rushing off to buy a house on a whim!

Hints & Tips for Longer Trips by Sylvia & Terry Cook

Whether you have invested in a holiday or retirement home in Greece or, like Anne and Ron Richardson you prefer to rent for the freedom to move and change plans, here are a number of tips and updates to help you plan and enjoy your stay in Greece. Many are useful if you move permanently too.

Keeping in Touch

It's good to keep in touch! In Greece you can collect your mail from the local post office which will have a place for *'post restante'* mail even if it's only a pile on a desk for people to look through. In villages where few streets have names or house numbers, your address will be your name plus the local post office address and postcode. If valuable packages or important documents are being sent it is worth paying the extra for 'signed for' delivery as mail can go astray. You could have someone redirect your UK mail to Greece, but we would suggest them opening it first and sending only relevant mail excluding envelopes and unnecessary 'bumph' as international postage is expensive these days. (You can always look through the catalogues, marketing literature and competition opportunities on your return.) A faster and more secure alternative if you have a computer and internet connection in Greece is via....

Email and Internet

A friend or family member could open and scan your mail to send to you via internet. You will need software that produces a very small file as connection speeds in Greece tend to be very slow. We use **e-fax** software where a mono page image is usually just 5kb to 25kb. E-fax is simple to use and free (download from www.efax.com) and you don't have to use their fax service.

Emails are a quick, cheap and an effective way to keep in touch. If you have a digital camera you can also send pictures of what you are getting up to. Remember to create a smaller version of your pictures for quicker internet transfer, reduce to a size you can see at 100% on the screen. It is also worth warning friends to reduce the size of pictures they send to you and ensure they are in compressed .tif, .jpg or .gif format for internet transfer (and ask them not to include you on lists for those 'round robin' emails with lots of pictures). We regularly get our email blocked in Greece by people trying to send large files. The system 'times out' after a few minutes so we can't get at subsequent emails without going to the service provider website and deleting the culprit.

You can access your UK email address in Greece via your provider's webmail at internet cafes. If you have your own phone line and computer you

can use a Greek Internet Service Provider. If your stay or requirements do not warrant the more expensive contract options, several companies provide pay-as-you-go card access at very cheap on-line rates, and with the flexibility of 'only when you need it'. OTE and Forthnet, as well as others, sell cards available through periptera or their offices from €3 to €20. You could, of course, get a Greek email address, but if you have a UK one, there's no need.

Telephone

To have a telephone installed at your house costs about the same as in the UK (subject to nearby existing lines), but the waiting time can be considerable unless, like us, you are lucky enough to go for one when there is a sales drive on - we got ours the following day! The internet cards mentioned above can also be used for telephone calls - you enter the card and PIN number at a house or public phone. An OTE standard phone card is also widely available for using public telephones, now plentiful in Greece. With some cards, any unspent value is forfeited at the end of an expiry period.

A money saving tip for friends in the UK to contact you in Greece, or for you when you want to call your Greek friends from the UK - for 5p per minute calls to Greece 24 hrs dial 0844 844 8444 from a UK land line, wait for the voice to confirm your call rate then dial the full Greek telephone number starting 0030 .... To call Greek mobile numbers for 15p per minute dial 0905 301 5301 first.

Mobile Telephones

It will be expensive to use your UK mobile phone in Greece, although some services provide for Greek calls at local rates plus a small premium. If you want to make a lot of local calls within Greece you can get a replacement chip with a Greek mobile telephone number to fit most modern UK mobile phones. Our Vodafone/Panafon replacement chip cost just €15 and included €8 of calls. Its UK equivalent 'pay as you go' telephone service chip cost £20 and included only £1 of calls. We bought ours in a mobile phone shop in Greece, but I understand they are also available in some supermarkets. The helpful assistant even installed it for us and set it up for English on screen help. When you return to the UK you just swap the UK chip back into the phone.

Money for Your Trip

We all know that Greece is generally a safe country, but your travel insurance is unlikely to cover you for large amounts of cash. Even with travellers cheques it is difficult to estimate how much you will need for a long stay and commission is paid on the full amount you take. You may need top ups during your stay if you are relying on a regular pension income. Remember that getting cash with a credit card attracts both a fee and interest from the day you withdraw it, which could prove very expensive. If there is a local branch or travelling bank where you are staying you can set up a Greek bank account and you may be lucky enough to have a local 'hole in the wall' to take money out as required. Beware that it may take some months to organise a card. The usual bank account offered is with a pass book, it pays a small interest but does not have a cheque facility, although other forms of account are available including internet banking. In Greece payment is generally expected in cash - even for buying a house!

You can arrange transfers of funds into your account by telephone or post from your UK bank account, but discuss this with your bank <u>before</u> you leave the UK. It is always worth requesting the **'pink slips'** on transfer to prove you brought the money into the country - especially if buying property or working in Greece as the authorities may otherwise assume you earned the money in Greece and are liable for tax on it.

A cautionary tale from John Corlett who purchased a house in Paros with his brother: *"The outcome of our case was that we finally fought off the Paros tax office's demand for £18K of tax, levied on grounds that my brother couldn't show he'd brought his money into Greece (because I'd brought it in for him!). But it took a very determined accountant who went to Athens on our behalf and wouldn't let go of the case. Our lawyer was worse than useless, having failed to advise us of the way to import money in the first place, and then charging us about £2K to fail to fix it afterwards!"*

Travel & Health Insurance

There are a number of companies offering annual or long term travel insurance, but it can be difficult to find at reasonable rates as you get older. Check the maximum length of trip on annual policies, many only allow 45 or 60 days maximum for an individual trip.

If you wish to stay more than 3 months in Greece, you need to register with the authorities (many still insist on a residence permit) to show you have the money or a job to support yourself. If you are not yet of retirement age, you may need to show that you have health insurance. This can be very expensive for long periods if organised from the UK, but you may find Greek Private Health Insurance cheaper. Treatment for holders of form E111 covers you only for a stay up to 3 months and in theory only for emergencies. You may find that paying privately for healthcare, dentistry, etc in Greece is cheaper than in the UK.

What to Bring from the UK

You can buy most things you will <u>need</u> in Greece - although not always as cheaply or with much choice of brands. You are bound to have a few personal favourite items that you will want to take (we always take cheaper instant coffee and cheddar cheese for the start of our visit), but flight weight limits and space availability mean you need to minimise these. Obviously if you are driving to Greece you will have more space, but do try to take advantage of the things that are cheaper in Greece and learn to manage with what IS available. Live the Greek life you have gone there for.

Camperdecks on Italy to Greece Ferries

We were told this useful spring to autumn facility (for staying in your own motorhome or caravan, or for pets with you to stay in your vehicle overnight) was being withdrawn due to new EU 'safety' rulings

in 2004. The individual companies' websites varied, so we booked through a UK agent believing they would have comparative information. We had to book a double cabin, adding greatly to our costs. Single sex 'dormitory' cabins or deck passage (not much comfort on a 22-24 hour crossing) are cheaper. Arriving at Ancona early April 2004 we were put on the Anek camper deck and could have slept in our caravan - no downgrade refund was available. Minoan Lines are also still offering a camperdeck and we understand it is only Superfast who have withdrawn the facility this year. It would seem better to book direct with the ferry company to get their latest facts.

Safety Checks Before Leaving

Unplug electric and telephone connections and turn power off at your fuse box. Another cautionary tale, from Marc Dubin who has had a house on Samos for some years. After reading about our fire he wrote *"I too had a fire in the place I was renting before moving into my restored house. Luckily the fire was contained to the corner where my fax machine was. I lived in the deflection range of a hilltop mobile telephone antenna, typically fitted with powerful lightning rods. I wasn't present, but apparently an almighty bolt of lightning hit the power pole near my isolated house and the charge travelled through all the electrical wiring of the house. I'd left the fax/answerphone plugged in. It exploded burning everything around it, causing much damage and loss, not to mention smoke damage throughout before the fire was put out. I would therefore strongly advise anyone leaving a Greek home for any length of time to unplug EVERY appliance, including the fax and telephones, as bolts can apparently travel up*

telephone wires too. You can fit a surge protector for items such as your refrigerator which could be on a separate fuse left switched on."

Back Home

If you are leaving your UK home empty for a long period, do leave a key with a trusted friend or family member to clear mail from the door and open or forward it. Tell your local police you will be away, who has access to your home and how you and they can be contacted. In most cases police are too busy to 'keep an eye' on your home these days, but in the event of an incident at least they will know the circumstances. Set lights to switch on and off at appropriate times in your absence so the house appears lived in to the casual passer-by. Check the maximum period of absence and any relevant sub-clauses with your home insurance provider.

Leaving Your Car in Greece - Update

We thought we had finally cracked this one! There are many information sources and for years various authorities have told us that unless you are a resident (when you can buy locally or pay a more realistic 20% of the high import tax to bring your own car in) you can only drive for 6 months per annum a UK/EU taxed and insured car (as stated in Vol 2), but you need to return to the UK for your annual MOT in order to re-tax it. We know information given by EU, British or Greek authorities or websites is sometimes out of date and local police/customs often interpret the rules differently. We finally found a ruling on a current Greek Ministry information site that confirmed tax free importation of your EU car for EU residents who do not stay in Greece more than 180 days in a year.

We drove down in our old Suzuki Samurai (UK value approx £1,000) intending to leave it in Greece. We had organised to de-register it in the UK (a legal requirement of the DVLA if it is to be out of the country for more than 12 months) and understood from helpful Athens Ministry of Finance sources that we would not need Greek registration for the first year. We checked with Mytilene customs shortly after our arrival who confirmed we could leave it at the port on exit, but we did not need to do anything until the day before our departure.

Great, we thought. All we needed was to organise Greek Car Insurance. Unfortunately, in 2004 Greece enacted the EU 4th Directive which requires vehicle insurance to be issued ONLY in the country of registration. We did discover, however, that by EU law, any motor insurance policy issued in the EU must include Third Party Legal Liability cover to drive in ALL EU countries. Only your additional cover (eg comprehensive) can restrict the number of days of overseas travel, or surcharge for additional days. The only prob-

lem was that our UK insurance could only work if the Suzuki was UK registered and taxed, which meant an annual return trip for the MOT, etc. We entered into a 'dialogue' (several visits and phone calls) with our local customs official in Mytilene through a very helpful lady, who worked in the canteen there, acting as interpreter.

We asked about Temporary Licence Plates (Red plates, although one Ministry said they were Green for the EU) which we needed to get Greek insurance, and the cost was not prohibitive - about €220 per annum including road tax. However, you have to get new plates every year and the vehicle must be 'sealed' by customs when you are not in Greece to validate the 6-month rule.

Fine - except the customs shed in Mytilene was full of cars on temporary import regulations and they refused to take any more! We were told we had to pay for them to come to our village to seal and unseal the car, and this could be up to a week prior to departure and after returning. Apart from the cost (up to €50 a visit) and the inconvenience, we would also still need costly taxis to and from the airport. Also a Greek friend must sign as guarantor to an unlimited sum (eventually they agreed a figure of €3,500 for our £1000 value car) in the event of us not complying with rules - which are not offered in writing (even in Greek) to ensure we understood what we must do.

The whole exercise was getting to be not worth the effort and expense! So although we did find a helpful hotel nearer the airport where we could leave the car, the bureaucracy surrounding temporary importation, in Lesvos anyway, became too cumbersome. We think we will drive the Suzuki back to the UK to sell it, and at a later date obtain a local residence permit and buy a second-hand Greek-registered car, which is now becoming a more widely available option and cheaper than before. (We've just found another possibility - as journalists/itinerant workers we are allowed to use our vehicle as long as we like in other EU countries, but we would still have the problem of needing an annual UK MOT for road tax as it would remain a UK registered vehicle ... and could we explain it to Mytilene Customs officials?)

It is hoped the EU will do something to end this nonsense of bureaucratic restrictions between European countries before long. Even their own website bemoans the fact that the prime EU right of freedom of movement of its citizens, can currently only be exercised for long periods WITHOUT the most common form of personal transport - your car!

Last Night on the Prom *by Sue Wardle*

It was late September, our last night on Crete. Billy and I had enjoyed two hot weeks in the south punctuated by an interesting and instant downpour which had taken us totally by surprise. However, that wasn't the only surprise we'd encountered.

We had dined at a taverna on the harbour-front whilst watching a superb sunset and were sorry to be leaving our favourite island with its beautiful scenery of rugged mountains and its long sandy beaches. Our day had been spent wandering around the village saying our last farewells. We had noticed posters nailed onto telegraph poles announcing that the local ladies were to provide an evening of food and dance. It sounded good, so after our meal we settled down with a beer at a table in front of a gyros shop to watch events develop.

By 10 pm trestle tables were arranged around the square loaded with meats, salads and cakes, all looking so inviting that we were quite sorry we had already eaten, although earlier we had made the decision not to overindulge the evening before our flight home. More tables and chairs arrived on anything that could transport them. Lines of lorries, vans, three-wheelers all deposited their loads in untidy heaps and then got in each other's way trying to turn round for the return trip. Total chaos. However, some sort of order eventually prevailed. Tables and chairs were arranged in neat rows and the square began to fill up with locals and tourists alike. Spare chairs piled high became the local children's playground and we watched with our hearts in our mouths as they leapt from stack to stack, squealing with laughter.

A stranger approached our table and asked to join us. We readily agreed and made instant friends with Rudolph, an Austrian biker who had spent several weeks travelling around Greece, stopping wherever he fancied. This was his last night too and we exchanged stories of our experiences and our favourite islands.

As we chatted, a lady passed by and Rudolph beckoned her over. Doris was a Swiss lady whom Rudolph had met earlier that day. She was meeting her German

Rudolf, Billy and Sue (me)

friends Jacob and Sue who arrived shortly after, followed by Otto and Hans with their friends. As the party grew we added more tables and chairs until we eventually stretched right across the road. By now drinks were flowing, eyes sparkling and cheeks becoming flushed. We had quite forgotten our earlier resolution and were prepared to take the consequences.

An announcement was made over a tannoy. We stood on our chairs to look over the sea of people and saw the mayor arrive, dressed in a white suit. The suit didn't appear to be his. The centre jacket button strained to fasten across his ample chest and the tight trousers stopped short of his winkle-picker shoes showing a large expanse of neon socks. However, he proudly stood on the makeshift stage and began a long speech, accompanied by many wild gestures of his arms and cheers from the crowd. After one final wave and applause from his audience, the music started and a troupe of young girls dressed in local costume began to dance. This was a chance not to be missed and I, rather unsteadily, made my way through the crowd with my camera.

My vacant seat!

Billy and our new friends continued to enjoy each other's company until a rather scruffy Greek man approached.

"Chair" he said, and went to remove my vacant seat.

"Οχι" said Billy (one of the few Greek words he knows) and waved him away.

The Greek was not to be deterred and tried to pull the chair away.

"Οχι!" said Billy more emphatically, taking hold of the chair and placing it down again. He waved to the stacks of unused chairs, indicating that the Greek should take one of those instead. The Greek muttered something under his breath and sat defiantly on the chair, insolently staring into Billy's face. The party of friends now became quite interested and all eyes were on the pair to see what would happen next.

"We fight for chair" said the Greek, putting his elbow on the table and holding his hand high. Billy was quite alarmed until he realised that an arm wrestle was intended. He put his arm on the table and grasped the Greek's hand. They both took the strain.

They sat for a short while staring each other out until the Greek, looking Billy up and down, snorted contemptuously and said *"You have more jewellery than my wife!"*

Billy released his grip and slowly removed his silver bracelet, silver rings and necklace and slammed them down on the table between them.

They again took their position. The strain began to tell on the Greek. He was sweating and shifting in his chair. He held a grubby cigarette in his mouth and he leant further and further forwards until the cigarette was almost in Billy's face.

Suddenly Billy moved forward and with his teeth grasped the cigarette, snatched it out of the Greek's mouth and spat it into the road. The Greek was taken by surprise and Billy took his opportunity to wrench the Greek's arm down onto the table. Our friends cheered and raised their glasses.

The Greek was stunned that he had lost. He looked up and asked *"You German?"*

"Oχı" replied Billy *"Scottish".*

"Ah - Braveheart. You are a man!" With that the Greek stood up, shook Billy's hand and disappeared. Within a few minutes a large ouzo arrived at the table. *"With the compliments of Giorgos"* said the waiter.

A moment later I returned. *"You don't know what you've missed."* I said. *"I've got some great photos of the mayor."*

Life on The Holy Mountain *by John Arnell*

Perhaps a sampling of champagne was having its inevitable effect but something induced me to take on the planning for the renovation and restoration of the historic footpaths of Mount Athos. As a member of the Friends of Mount Athos, my wife and I were attending a reception being held by our patron, His Royal Highness, the Prince of Wales at Highgrove.

How did we come to be there? I had visited Mount Athos several times, more as an explorer than a pilgrim and had seen the ancient paths, once the prime means of communication and supply between the monasteries, slowly being bulldozed out of existence as the means of transport moved from mule to Land Rover and truck. The Prince of Wales had visited the Holy Mountain on a number of occasions too and was equally concerned. That led to his suggestion that the Friends should take this project in hand, to ensure the ancient footpaths are recorded, preserved and where necessary and possible, restored for the benefit of future generations.

Mount Athos occupies the most easterly of the three peninsulas that extend from Halkidiki in northern Greece into the Aegean. Known in Greece as Agio Oros, the Holy Mountain, the whole peninsula, between 5 and 8 miles wide, 35 miles long, is solely an Orthodox monastic community, from which women historically and to this day are excluded.

To visit the Holy Mountain means to experience, if not share, the demanding timetable of the monks. They are up at 3 am to pray for an hour, in the church from 4 until 9 am, then each monk has his role for the upkeep of the monastery - carpenter, farmer or manual labourer - which continues until noon. A monk's habit is not designed for manual labour in the Greek sun, hence a well earned rest follows until 4 pm when they are called to the church for a further service until 7 pm. Two vegetarian meals are provided each day as part of the church service. These are taken in silence, apart from listening to a reading from the scriptures intoned in Greek or the language of the monastery.

There are 20 monasteries, Greek, Russian, Roumanian, Serbian. Many of the younger monks in the Greek monasteries are returned emigrants to Australia, Canada or the USA. Add to these Orthodox monks from many of

Simonas
Monastery

the countries of Europe, including the UK and you find a surprising mixture of nationalities amongst the some 2000 monks that live and pray there. In addition to the monasteries, there are smaller communities of monks called *'skete'* and a

number of monks living as hermits in small *'kellion'* clinging to the cliffside at the Eastern end of the peninsula where Mount Athos itself plunges from its peak of 6600 ft to the sea.

The Athonite approach to the recording of time is complex. For some monasteries 12 o'clock is set at sunset, others set it at sunrise. Add to this the use of the Julian calendar that is 13 days behind the calendar we know and it all becomes very confusing.

The monasteries are 10th or 11th century in origin although many have been ravaged by fire over the years. Today they seem like a time capsule of some bygone age with treasures beyond belief. I have been close enough to touch, but did not, Ptolemy's 13th century BC map of Macedonia. It is awe inspiring to see something so old, so fragile and yet there for the pages to be turned and to be studied. One library is reputed to have over 2000 books and manuscripts kept safe by a number of complimentary keys which must be operated simultaneously to gain entry.

Even on Athos where time seems to have stood still, some aspects of life have changed. In an article entitled, 'The Orthodox Understanding of Pilgrimage' (Forerunner 38, Winter 2001-2) Bishop Kallistos of Diokleia, President and chairman of the Executive Committee of The Friends of Mount Athos, wrote: *I count it a singular blessing that I was able to visit the Holy Mountain of Athos first of all in autumn 1961, and again in autumn 1962, at*

a time when there were no roads for vehicles, no buses, no jeeps or tractors. ... As a pilgrim, either one travelled from monastery to monastery by the little motorboats that plied along the coast (but in the equinoctial gales most of these had been cancelled); or else one hired a mule (but that was far too expensive for a student like myself); or else one walked. I walked. At times it was hard work, for the ancient mule tracks of Athos are steep and stony. I lost my way, slipped into ravines, fell backwards into a thorn bush and twisted my ankle. But by walking alone meeting only the occasional monk, not to mention an alarming number of snakes and at one point a family of wild boar, I was able to experience Mount Athos as a centre in sacred space, in a way that otherwise I could not possibly have done. I was able to feel, in the words of the Russian Athonite hermit Fr. Nikon, "Here every stone breathes prayers".

For the last three years, I have taken a small group of volunteers, armed with saws, loppers, many pairs of gloves and such 'goodies' as the modest diet there has suggested we take along. In this time, we have cleared some 30 km of overgrown path and surveyed a further 80 km. The work is physically demanding especially in hot weather, although so far our visits have been shortly after Orthodox Easter, *Paskha*, in April or May. We have also been mapping the footpaths with simple GPS devices and some clever software. It is hoped this will lead to a detailed and accurate map becoming available over the next year or so.

A typical working day for the 'Footpath Warriors' starts with an early call at about 4 am to join the monks at prayers in the Katholikon, the central chapel. A gentle knock on the door and a softly announced *"Khristos Anesti"*, (Christ

The team take a well earned break -Vatopedi

is risen), might get the response *"Alithos Anesti"* (Truly He has risen) from anyone awake in the dormitory, but we generally stir before 6 am for a very hearty breakfast. By hearty, I include eggs, fish, some substantial pasta dishes and frequently wine, a major assault on a digestive system which is at best only half awake. By 7 am we are under way in whatever transport is available to get us close to our workplace, then up to a 40-minute hike uphill to where we finished working on the previous day.

We work in groups moving along the path, cutting and clearing a way. It's hard and thirsty work and by 1 pm we are ready for a break. We have a packed lunch prepared by the monks with a selection of olives, eggs, feta, nuts, oranges and some very substantial bread. Halva is usually provided but in quantities that after two weeks can induce a lifetime aversion to it. We work on until 3 or 4 pm before walking back to our transport. There is then a dash for the shower, hopefully warm, perhaps a few minutes of contemplation in the Katholikon before joining the monks for supper. This is taken in silence apart from one monk reading a passage from the scriptures, interrupted from time to time by the Abbot who addresses the monks in quite strident tones. We thought the reader was getting a telling off for some point but then realised the Abbot was elaborating on the reading.

The evening provides an opportunity to talk with the monks, discuss work plans and other more general or personal issues. The monastic life offers the opportunity to reflect on many of the world's problems and monks often show both perception and sensitivity in their views. They are well informed and aware about the world outside and make every use of computer technology in their planning and management. The evening is also an opportunity to see the treasures of the monastery and catch up with personal chores. By 9 pm we are in our dormitory with lights out by 10 pm.

We have been joined for a few days on each trip by His Royal Highness who has turned his hand to sawing and clearing along with the rest of the party. This is a task akin to painting the Forth Bridge, which will never be completed, but the opportunity to live and work in a monastic community is sufficient reward if indeed any reward is necessary.

The Holy Mountain is unique. Living and working there is a very special and personal experience. You realise the depth of its impact when, after two weeks, you return to your everyday life and notice how bright, noisy and almost garish it is.

The best of the many books on Athos and its history I've seen is *Mount Athos: Renewal in Paradise* by Graham Speake (Yale University Press). The Internet also provides details of Mount Athos and protocols necessary to visit. More details of the Footpath Restoration Project and the Friends of Mount Athos can be found at www.athosfriends.org.

The Taverna *by Pete Wolstencroft*

What looks like a miniature stovepipe hat, such as that worn by Abraham Lincoln, is brought to our table. But this one is made of pinkish metal and has a handle. It contains a litre of white wine, which when poured turns out to be a good deal nearer to brown than white. Skinny cats rub their necks on our ankles and strike poses they know to be popular with tourists. Considering the amount of juicy titbits they get through, it is nothing short of a miracle that they are so scrawny.

Photo by Sylvia Cook

The cicadas wind down for the evening and the crickets start on the night shift, ensuring that there is always a soundtrack. The backbeat is provided by the steady click-click of worry beads. The men - and it always seems to be men - wielding them look as if they have no concept of what it means to worry.

As the night sky turns inky black the geckoes come out. Opalescent bodies topped off with jet-black eyes. They are on our side: avid consumers of flies and mosquitoes. Bats too flit in and out of the canopy of branches above our heads. Old olive trees and vines are worked into the very fabric of the buildings, not encumbrances but rather centrepieces, sign posts indicating national and local identity.

There's a wellhead in the corner of the establishment, although fresh water has long since issued forth from taps just as it does back home. Wooden yokes for oxen and leather harnesses for donkeys, shiny from years of use, vie for wall space with religious icons and wooden shovels that presumably have some culinary function. The wickerwork chairs stick to the skin of your thighs, so that when you stand up at the end of a long lazy dinner, your chair comes with you - grafted to your backside with your own sweat!

Women, well past the first flush of youth, are sweating over glowing coals which sizzle noisily as the fat from the meat drips onto the charcoal below. Occasionally someone uses a hairdryer on the coals to bring them back up to maximum heat. Old men sit in corners drinking ouzo with their friends and directing operations with a nod of the head here, a raising of the chin there.

Tables at the water's edge fill up first. The night is filled with the scent of jasmine and bougainvillea and strangely enough, the cigarette smoke that so annoys me back home seems to stimulate the appetite here. Waiters clap you on the back as if to congratulate you for even the most elementary use of their language. Knives and forks come in a basket of bread and the wine glasses remind me of the water glasses from my primary school. Some of them even explode in the same way. I never did understand that phenomenon.

The souvlaki meat is so tender and juicy I suspect the pig may well have died of happiness. A waiter asks *"How do you say 'Kali Orexi' in English?"* *"Well actually it's not something we generally say"* I reply, feeling embarrassed. Back home I don't particularly like yoghourt or cucumber, so how is it that I can't get enough of tzatziki? When the waiters suggest a dish, you get the impression that you really don't have too much choice in the matter. Never mind, just go with the flow.

Need a map of the local area? Just sit right down and order some food. The paper cloth that will be brought to your table will be as good a map as you will need. The Spanish dine late, but in the late dinner stakes they are mere beginners. The Greeks think nothing of sitting down to eat at eleven thirty, and they are certainly not going to eat and run. Why would anybody want to rush?

Ouzo on its own - €1. Ouzo with something to eat - €2.5. Oh yes - ouzo and octopus: a great combination. But am I alone in thinking it just a little bit strange to have octopus hanging out to dry above the heads of the diners?

Photo by Sylvia Cook

Serried ranks of them speared in place by the hollow aluminium tubing that holds the canvas steady against the wind. Pity the poor cephalopod family; nearly all its members are here. Squid and cuttlefish complete the trio.

Peppers, onions, tomatoes, garlic and parsley all burst with flavour. Dill and wild oregano blend with cheese and meat juices. Bread is used as a sponge to wipe up every last drop. No meal is complete without watermelon, which comes unbidden, sometimes along with another stovepipe of wine. *"Excuse me, we didn't order this..."* Oh well, needs must when the devil drives!

Greek Winters *by Sylvia Cook*

Winters in Greece are different from the British experience, but don't be fooled into thinking that it is warmer further south. World weather patterns are changing so it is difficult to generalise and say this month or that month is the wettest, the coldest or the least hospitable. That's probably why there are few tour operators who organise trips to Greece outside the Spring to Autumn period.

Certainly the Greek cold and rainy spell is shorter than in Britain and weather changes occur very quickly. You could be enjoying sunning yourself at *'misimeri'* well into November and suddenly one day it will turn very cold, or the heavens will open and it will rain for days on end, **really** rain so that summer streets become rivers and dirt track roads are washed away. Likewise you may be experiencing cool or wet weather in Spring while in Britain they are enjoying a heatwave - but then one day the wind will turn and the seemingly endless days of summer begin again.

Mainland Greece is very mountainous and regularly experiences prolonged spells of sub zero temperatures. You may be surprised to know that Greece has a number of mainland ski resorts, although the best times for skiing may be difficult to predict. But that suits the Greek who can decide on a whim, when the snow is good, to spend a weekend skiing in Parnassos near Delphi, Helmos in the Peloponnese, Vermion, Metsovo, Pisoderi or other snow covered mountains where ski lifts are in place.

The islands of the Northeast Aegean are close to Turkey and the central land mass of Europe, and therefore affected by the sub zero conditions regularly experienced there. But even the most southerly major island, Crete, has snow regularly. Lefka Ori is not called white mountain for nothing! Recent winters have been exceptionally bad with Greece experiencing more snow in all parts than much of Britain. Trees and flowers which are not suited to

over-wintering in UK gardens *can* survive for many years (eg geraniums), but many lemon, orange and even olive groves died or will take several years to recover after the prolonged freezing conditions of winters in Greece from 2002 to 2004.

Fish lunch with feline 'waiters', Tavari Harbour

Although we have yet to experience a whole winter in Greece, we enjoy our winter trips to our island for several reasons. Unless the weather conditions are exceptionally severe we spend more time outside in the open in Lesvos, but wearing more and thicker layers of clothes to keep ourselves warm in often biting winds and freezing conditions. And yet other days the wind drops and the sun shines, so we can strip off a few layers and sit outside a kafeneion at lunchtime in short sleeves feeling the sun's warmth on our pale winter skins (alongside anoraked Greek friends). By 2-3 pm though the layers are gradually going back on, or we retreat inside to sit around a stove, as the temperature outside drops with the sun.

The quality of Greek light is renowned - but in the many clear days of a Greek winter it surpasses the often hazy, summer version. There is a crisp clarity to the skyline and islands which are not often visible in the summer haze appear as if from nowhere, much closer on the horizon. We flew into Mytilene at dawn one Winter's morning and I was amazed to look out and see a map of the North Aegean islands and Turkish coastline clearly laid out in front of us as the sun rose from the east.

However, when it does snow, villages can be cut off, deliveries and travelling banks do not arrive, taxis will not take chances - but in true Greek style there is 'okhi provlema'. Adults and children alike take to the streets and plateia to build snowmen or throw snowballs. It seemed odd to us that most built their snowmen on tables or on car bonnets.

In the winter everyone has more time to chat as village tavernas are rarely full and we get more chance to practise our Greek and learn new vocabulary. Although my grammar does not improve, fortunately our Greek friends have patience to try to understand! These days even the nearby beach resort has one or two businesses open in winter and it is good to pop down to watch the sea crashing in, feel the wind on our faces or enjoy a Greek coffee sat outside on a sunny winter's day.

When our house was being rebuilt in February 2003 we stayed in a friend's studio, built for summer use. It was VERY cold with thin breeze block walls, cold floors and a serious condensation problem. We needed to spend much of our time in kafeneia and tavernas to keep warm. I think that was the only time we were really pleased to be returning to UK. Do check if the property you are staying in is appropriate for winter life before you commit yourself.

A second cold snap in Eresos in January 2004 came after a blizzard and very strong winds (typhoon force recorded!), so everything was seriously frozen for a few days in our village. Many water supply pipes, including our own recently renewed meter and supply pipe, enter the premises above ground. We were without water one night and assumed it was the same throughout the village (we often have water and electricity cuts) until discovering our neighbour still had hers in the morning. Fortunately an electric blow heater trained on the offending frozen (hard plastic) pipe resolved the problem in less than half an hour. We lagged it and we were OK from then on. Higher in the village they were less fortunate and without a water supply for about 5 days  as frozen pipes had burst in many places. Getting a plumber is difficult enough in Eresos, without additional natural disasters! We didn't go out for 3 evenings in a row as the evening chill froze the river of rain and melted snow running down our street *(above)*, making it quite treacherous.

The first morning of snow after the freeze Alekos telephoned while we drank our first coffee of the day in bed at 8.30 am. Alekos told Terry, *"You must come down now. Tell Sylvia to bring her camera."* We dressed warmly and went down, using odd bits of wood as walking sticks to steady us, me snapping away at the incredible winter wonderland with icy snow balanced high on even the thinnest branches.

It took a good while to melt the snow on the trees and the next day most parts were still white, but the sun was shining. We were invited to visit and photograph a waterfall by Panayotis, owner of the land around it. Driving in his Suzuki Vitara once off the main Eresos to Andissa road the track was slippery and dangerous. We insisted on getting out to trudge through the snow on foot and were well rewarded after a few kilometres hike. The waterfall was magnificent *(bottom centre on front cover)*, two falls into a deep lake then a third alongside an old water mill. They say the water falls there all year round. It's good walking country which we enjoyed revisiting with friends in the warmer weather of May. Surprisingly few people know of the existence of the Megga Lakkos waterfall, even fewer have seen it.

Somehow we always find different things to do or unusual places to go in winter. It seems easier to get involved when people have more time to spare, so we'll go on enjoying at least a part of every winter in Greece.

Tails from The National Gardens *by Mary Cochrane*

(& Kili)

(In memory of Kyriako, Ancient One, Mrs. Ear, the Mavroaspri and all the other Garden cats, whether they lived there for just a few hours or, occasionally, for long and happy lives)

MIEOOOW!

I'm Kili and I live in the National Gardens here in Athens. My friends and I heard that the last volume of Greek-o-File included an article on Athenian street dogs and we thought that it was about time that us cats made our side of the story heard too. As I seem to have been appointed 'spokescat' for the Gardens (I write a popular column in the Friends of the Cat Magazine, more about them later) I was nominated to 'put you in the picture'.

Well, first of all, let me introduce myself. I am one of the longer-term residents here. I am a very handsome, though I say it myself, silver tabby, possibly slightly on the portly side but then I *do* like my food. I was dumped some five years ago and I must say I found things very difficult at first - *'Where is my food and water?' 'Why does no-one pay me any attention?' 'Why are all those other cats trying to eat my food?' 'Why won't they let me have some?' 'What are all these dogs doing here and why do they want to kill me?'* and *'Now that I've got away from them, just how do I get down from this tree?'*

Anyway, I got the hang of things a bit, and despite a slight accident which left me with a hernia, I must say that I manage here a lot better than most of the other poor souls. And, of course I am well looked after - I am fed every day without fail, vaccinated once a year and I was even given some wonderful medicine when I had a most troublesome and persistent problem with ear-mites. And of course I was taken off to be neutered soon after I arrived here - in fact all us gardens cats are neutered and although, as a male, I wasn't too keen on the idea at first, I have to admit that the last thing we need here is lots of kittens (and life is just a lot more laid back without all that fighting and spraying nonsense).

However, you are not just interested in me - and my brief is to try and let you know something about our life here in general.

Well - where to begin? First of all, we are all abandoned pets with our own stories to tell and our own personalities. That may surprise some of you who have met our feral cousins who have never been 'owned' where they live and scavenge in island and mainland villages, but here in the city a number of charities have helped us over many years with neutering programmes and cut down on unwanted pregnancies. Some of us have never really forgiven people for abandoning us and don't really want much to do with them any more, while others spend all their time trying to persuade passers-by to take them home (occasionally it works - one of my best friends now lives in *Paris* of all places, after having done a particularly charming routine on a passing French family). In fact, even if they don't take us home, tourists provide hours of excellent entertainment.

Tourist-spotting is one of our favourite occupations, especially in summer. There is something wonderfully relaxing about lying here in the shade and watching them stagger by in the full noon heat, laden down with video cameras, rucksacks and maps. Actually, they seem to spend an inordinate amount of time peering at their maps trying to find the Kalimarmaro, the Acropolis or the toilets (especially the toilets). And we occasionally have a bit of a wager on what nationality will pass by next - at the moment my bet is on a British family but my best friend Carlos is convinced that it will be a party of Russian businessmen. We used to try our *'starving-Greek-cat'* act on the more cat-friendly looking tourists, just in case they had a particularly tasty titbit but it didn't often work. They just kept looking at us and saying *'my, aren't they fat and healthy'*. We used to try and explain that this is because we are so well looked after, but between you and me, tourists are a bit slow on the uptake and they would start stroking us and saying *'and aren't they friendly too!'* Now, we are always happy to be stroked and made a fuss of, but, sooner or later, some tourist would nearly always point out that Carlos doesn't have a tail, something he is a bit sensitive about as it was the result of a nasty encounter with a stray dog some years ago. In the end we give up on the tourists and just concentrate on eating and keeping cool.

But life here is not all tourist-spotting. There's work to do. Us old hands have quite a job trying to make sure the new *'dumpees'* fit in and get along with everyone. Some of them adapt fairly easily but there are some poor souls who don't ever really seem to get over the shock of being dumped. Take Stringla for instance, she has been in a permanent bad mood since she was left here three years ago - she even had a serious falling out session with the food-bag today (there is definitely something wrong with this

Stringla

cat - she can't even be civil to her food….). And then there is Mad Asterioti and Esmeralda - now I'm not one to gossip, but some of us have more robust mental health than others - Esmeralda thinks she is a duck (poor dear) and Mad Asterioti,

Mad Asterioti

while perhaps slightly more stable, is still not quite the full shilling, but she's recently found a new home and owner to care for her - bless her.

And then we had another (I must admit heart-rending) example of female sensitivity - this time with a happy ending. Poor 'Mana' was dumped last year with two kittens. The ever-caring Friends of the Cat found a home for Shy but the other little one grew up in the Gardens. All went well, his mother doted on him - imagine - when she was sterilized she even took him with her to stay at the vet's, but one day tragedy struck. I hardly need say - dogs again. Poor Mana was inconsolable and terrified. She went and hid in a dark, damp underground pipe and didn't come out again for FIVE months. Five winter months in a cold, wet pipe! All her hair fell out and she was as thin as anything (shame really because she had been a real pretty wee thing). The kind Friends of the Cat people were persistent. They used to call and call at the mouth of the pipe until eventually she would answer them and slowly, slowly make her way out. But while she was happy out with her human friends, rubbing herself against their feet and purring, the minute they got up to go she would disappear back into that pipe. In the end they couldn't stand it any longer and, after months of trying, found her a home. Her hair grew back, she got positively fat and we all envied her good luck (even if she did earn it the hard way).

Now, I am sure you all know how things work here in Greece and we cats have to look after our own interests just as much as anyone else. So, it will not surprise you to know that my faithful feeder and I struck a mutually beneficial deal involving several tins of my very favourite cat food this morning. And as I am an honourable cat I have to keep my end of the bargain and give a good plug to Friends of the Cat's 'Sponsor a Stray' scheme. (Actually, I would willingly have done this anyway as they do try their hardest to look after you, but if one can negotiate a few extra yummy meals then why not?).

Well, anyway, if you would like to help them to look after cats like us all over Greece then maybe you could sponsor one of their rescued strays? For £8 a month you can help them keep an ex-street cat safe and warm (and fat!) and in return they will send you a sponsorship pack with photos of 'your cat' (this is Evgadzi who is looking for a sponsor as I dictate this) and you receive a newsletter in English to keep you up to date with things here.

Full details of the sponsorship programme can be found on their website friendsofthecat.com or, if you don't like to get involved with those 'computer' things, you can write to them at FRIENDS OF THE CAT, PO BOX 18192, PANGRATI, 116 01, ATHENS, GREECE and they will send you an information sheet on the sponsorship programme and on the work they do here. And, if you don't fancy the regular commitment of sponsoring a stray they are always happy to receive ad hoc donations (sterling is no problem). I should perhaps point out that I am on commission here (an especially yummy tin of food for every cat sponsored and for every donation received) so rest assured that anything you can give will be *doubly* appreciated.

Ah, Carlos has just nudged me to point out a group of Russian business-men strolling by. I think I will have to wander over and check that they really are Russian. You never know. .... Well, never mind - and I was *sure* I was on to a winner.

Adopting Mini *by John Thorogood*

It was late September 2002 and we had just arrived on a 2 week charter, staying at our regular hotel in Haramida, a gaggle of houses and a couple of hotels and tavernas on the spectacular winding coast road about 7 kms beyond Mytilene airport. We headed straight for the beach and the familiar greeting from Fanis and Barbara who run the 'Kantina' on this wide stony beach (the sand was taken away by the Colonels to build the new runway at Mytilene airport). It is very popular with the locals - but not many tourists find it.

There are always stray dogs running around and on this day a small fluffy terrier pup ran up to us and plonked herself on my towel as if she owned it. She and her friend 'Flock' amused themselves by chasing cars on the dirt road behind the beach.

A few days later Barbara told me that her dog, Flock, had been knocked down and killed by a car - so Mini (as we called her, after a local ouzo brand) was left on her own. She was not in good shape at all - canker in both ears, ticks, matted fur etc. She had also broken a leg at some point although this was not obvious as the bone had set itself, albeit not in the same place as before. We had pretty well decided that Mini would have to come back to England with us (the alternatives seemed to be starvation, sudden death by motor vehicle or shooting by the local shepherds).

After numerous phone calls we found a temporary home for her in nearby Alifanda where a delightful couple own a 6000 sq.ft villa and about 20 dogs. Eva met us at midnight before our departure and she then arranged for Mini to have shots and medical treatment and made arrangements with a shipper at Spata airport in Athens to transport Mini to Gatwick. We had meanwhile arranged for her to be met at Gatwick by the Lady Haye kennels where she went straight into quarantine for 6 months.

After weekly visits from November onwards we finally brought her home on 8th May 2003, much to the disgust of our 6 cats. It was a costly exercise, but one we would repeat again if the occasion arose. Mini now has a pet passport so we may make the journey back to Mytilene by car one day and see if she remembers her roots.

Mini enjoying her new pampered life

Toilet Talk *by Jenny Booth*

Whenever Greek toilets are mentioned it is often with an air of *'say no more!'*. Now call us sad if you like but Colin and I like to *'score'* the loos. This was taught to us by an older couple we met on one of our early trips, who had been going to Greece for many years. We used to meet regularly in a bar which had a particularly awful loo which was how it became a topic of conversation.

Now when we visit an establishment for the first time whoever goes to the loo first returns and says a number, usually between one and ten. This is the loo score. It goes something like this.

One point for each of the following:

'Lavatory' Photo Sylvia Cook

- Can you find the light switch?
- Does the door shut ? and if so does it lock?
- Is it clean enough (advice is not to look too closely)?
- Is there a loo seat - attached to the loo ? (actually sitting on it is not compulsory)
- Is there any loo paper?
- Has the bin been emptied in the last —hours/days (insert a figure to suit your own levels of hygiene/optimism)?
- Can you fathom where the flush mechanism is and does it work?
- Is there anywhere to wash your hands?
- Soap?
- Drying facility? (OK, I know I'm stretching it a bit here).

Minus points can be scored in respect of the following:

- Distance of the loo from the taverna (memories of long walks up dark back alleys!).
- and the opposite.... Proximity to the food preparation area.
- Assault on olfactory organ.
- Does paddling become necessary at any point in the proceedings?

Oh yes, and

- that not infrequent missing panel of frosted glass which means that despite the door locking anyone standing outside has a perfect view of you going about your business!

Bonus points can be given at your discretion for loos which are so good they make you wonder whether you are still in Greece.

Then there are points (plus or minus, as you see fit) for such idiosyncrasies as part of the door having been hacked away to ensure it clears the pedestal as it opens, and can you squeeze round it if you are an ounce fatter than Victoria Beckham?

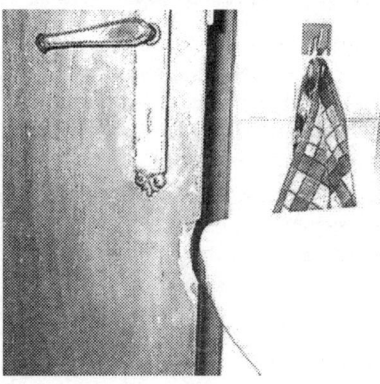

Photo by M Dowle

Anything close to 10 is considered outstanding and worth making a detour for a quick drink and loo visit another day, but I'm sure you will not be surprised to learn that we have been to places which have large minus scores. It also has to be said that the general appearance of the taverna or bar often bears no relation to the state of the loo. Also, perversely, some of the grottiest will have a row of cleaning materials stashed in the corner. Are they ever used?

The scoring system is flexible and can be made up as you go along to suit your personal preferences, likes and dislikes.

(If Arthur Deeks & Harry get to read this I'm sure they could make a valuable contribution as there is probably further technical plumbing detail which has passed me by.)

Notes from editor: Greek People are often nonplussed by British 'Toilet Humour' and may not appreciate that Jenny's loo scoring can be fun! Most regular visitors have come to terms with putting paper in the bin, and have learned to accept that 'out of the way' places may not have the latest plumbing or frequent cleaning. Jenny's points system formalises what I imagine a number of us have been doing for years - asking "What are the loos like?" of the first person who visits the 'toualetta'. At least this system avoids graphic details being discussed over food and drink.

Photo by Sylvia Cook

The dreaded 'footpad' loo (especially awkward for females wearing shorts) still to be found in some old village and town kafeneia. This one was reasonably clean and fresh (harbour taverna Kissamos, Crete 2000) unlike the one I encountered on my first ever trip to Greece in 1975 on a mainland coach drive (Corfu to Athens) which was definitely a minus 10.

Shopping CAN be a Pleasure! *by Michael Saunders*

Pauline and I live in a mountain village in Western Crete where life meanders by without any jostle and hassle – until we need to go shopping for something more than everyday needs. So it was, with a shopping list prepared, earmarking bank, opticians, curtain rail ends and lighting, I prepared to be scrambled, ready to hit the big city – Chania. I don't mind one stop shopping in a supermarket, but struggling to find somewhere to park, and traipsing about in the heat, is not my favourite cup of tea.

We descended from the solitude and clear mountain air into the roar and acrid fumes of cheek by jowl cars and buses in the city. Here, proud car owners always park with their wing mirrors folded back. With narrow streets, two lines of traffic and cars parked either side; there is a mathematical formula which equates to the average vehicle having twenty centimetres of free space port and starboard. Stray from this line and you hit something. Peering either side I began hunting for a space - only to be thwarted many times by a chair, guarding an expected forthcoming delivery, or a moped standing in oceans of space, cocking a thumb at drivers who could have parked there.

"There's one!"

I jammed on the brakes. The car behind screeched. Traffic ground to a halt. I opted for the Greek system of parking. To do this you have to blithely ignore the cacophony of honking, which you are the cause of, and the other drivers' furious gesticulations. With confusion reigning, I attempted to jiggle and joggle the car into a ridiculously small space. Finally, perfectly parked, Greek style, a metre from the kerb and a centimetre from a clutch of scooters fore and aft, we emerged from our air conditioned cocoon into the dusty, cloying heat and traffic returned to normal.

First call, was the bank, as you can't shop without money. This was the big city and bartering with eggs for something doesn't appear to work here!

We bank at the Agrotiki - the farmer's bank. I don't know whether having eight olive trees, and keeping chickens, ducks and turkeys makes me a farmer, but I like the Agrotiki. The service we receive knocks spots off any UK bank. Ianna, behind the counter, smiled and offered us tiropitas. *"They are fresh; my Mother cooked them this morning."*

"Would you like a biscuit?" called out the Chief Clerk.

Could you go into Barclays or NatWest and be offered coffee and snacks, while the clerk counts out cash and the old villager behind you has a gun slung over his shoulder?

We emerged with our spending money. Pauline set stride for Andreos' shop.

"Why go to the opticians," I moaned. *"There's a choice of hundreds at every tourist shop AND they're cheaper!"*

I followed Pauline's sniff of disdain with all the petulance of a grumbling schoolboy set for a long, boring wait. Andreos, the optician, must have thought I looked despondent, for I was given a tray of peanuts, glasses and tsikouthia (local raki) to keep me amused - and a very good job it did too. Time seemed to flash by, with only the occasional interruption of being asked for an opinion on a particular style.

"Mm, they're OK," I'd reply with a well worn sigh, only to receive a barbed, *"Well, you could at least try to look interested!"*

Dusk was falling as, purchase finally made, we walked along the street to the hardware shop, where Pauline wanted to buy curtain rail ends, and a whole host of other strange things, I knew not what.

The shop owner sat behind the till, while his wife and Pauline meandered around the shop, in deep discussion.

"Tsikouthia?"

I had obviously met a kindred spirit. Out came an innocent bottle of Sprite and a saucer of biscuits. I was beginning to enjoy shopping.

Another happy half-hour sped by, before I staggered out with three large bags of assorted bits and pieces, all destined for numerous jobs to be done at home. Thankfully we did not have far to go - next door to the lighting shop.

Vangelis and Ismene welcomed us with open arms. I sat down, the women discussed what was to be purchased and Vangelis made a telephone call, before winking and producing a bottle of Coke, one of Sprite and two plastic

beakers. I had a choice – tsikouthia from grapes, or tsikouthia from mulberries. I chose the latter. Well, it made a change.

With beaker charged, we toasted each other and downed the spirit in one. My cauterised tonsils screamed and charred taste buds gasped for breath. This was truly a drink to sort the men from the boys. As my system gradually returned to normal, smooth, musky flavours came to the fore, which tasted really rather pleasant the more you drank.

This was obviously a five-star establishment in my Rough Guide to Shopping, for Vangelis brought out a huge wedge of cheese, cut into generous pieces with his knife. A plate of honey appeared, followed by one of tomatoes – and then, in response to the phone call made to the kafeneion down the street, came cheese pies and a plate of grilled jacket potatoes sprinkled with lemon juice.

It was now nine thirty and most shops were closed. Pauline had bought some garden lights and all was well in my world.

Vangelis and I were now bosom buddies and at his insistence, we staggered out into the street, down to a minuscule kafeneion. It was only just over two metres wide and inside a long table was set, at which sat more than twenty people. It was a party! All the shops along the street had an annual celebration and tonight was the night! The table groaned under the weight of food, as we all tucked in. Music played, beer and wine flowed freely, tonsils became ever more lubricated and conversation became faster and louder above the blare of music.

At half past one in the morning we, or rather I, staggered to the car and as Pauline drove home, the last thing I remembered before drifting off, was that I really liked this shopping lark. We should do it more often.

What Do They Talk About ? *by Alison Graddon*

What do they talk about?
Two grey-haired women on a pebbled Greek beach.
They sit together every evening
once the village comes to life and the warm breeze
filters the afternoon heat.

One is thin and wiry and all in black,
the other stocky in black, but
with some relief in a patterned
square-cut top.
Somehow traditional, part of the local scene.

They stay until the last excursion boat has been and gone
returning visitors to their cars or coaches.
They stay until the first of the small blue painted fishing boats goes out
beyond the harbour walls.

So animated, they point at times beyond
the overseeing mountains
towards hill villages and scattered relics of a more prosperous time.

What do they talk about?

A new baby is brought to the shore while they are there
to be shown to all, but especially grandfather
mending his saffron coloured nets.
The women stop talking and look and smile.
It sets off further thoughts and lively chat.

When the heatwave arrived there was more discussion.
The black thick stockings were rolled down, then taken off.
Together the ladies entered the water,
still talking.

But what do they talk about?

(Ormos, Samos July 2003)

This section is a collection of personal experiences (some could be anywhere in Greece), views and research, with maps and an overview profile accompanying the main travel reports. The articles entertain, inform, offer a personal viewpoint which may suggest your kind of destination, or just remind you of similar incidents or places you have enjoyed. First, Mrs Woodhouse was reminded of one special moment when reading an earlier volume and wrote to tell us.

Olympia, A Place in My Heart *by M C Woodhouse*

About fifteen years ago we took a day excursion to Olympia from Kefalonia. On arrival the site was extremely busy and the weather very hot, but what an impression it made. The atmosphere was great.

At the actual race track I had the urge to run the course where the ancient Greeks had competed all those years before. But in the heat no one was even standing on it. Crowds of visitors and my own inhibitions prevented me.

Over the years this was my greatest regret. The thought *"I wish I'd at least stood on the track at Olympia"* kept coming into my mind.

Then two years ago we revisited Kefalonia with our grandaughter and other members of the family. Of course we just **had** to go back to Olympia. This time people were walking on the track and I thought *"Now's my chance"*. So the ladies in our party lined up - half way down the track as the temperature was 40°C. *"Ready, steady, go!"*

What a great feeling. Emotion and elation ending with laughter. *"I did it, I did it"* was all I could say as I reached the finish line. NOW I can say I have run on the original Olympic track.

Why it became so important to me, I can't explain, or why Greece has found a place in my heart, **it just has.**

Kalavrita, A Lasting Impression by Kenneth MacColl

When we booked for the tour all we had in mind was a day away from the beach. Our courier had spoken of a leisurely coach trip through Arcadia and the rural scenery that name evoked, along with a spectacular downhill ride on the rack and pinion railway from **Kalavrita** (Καλάβρυτα), high on the plateau, to **Diakofto** (Διακοφτό) on the shores of the Gulf of Corinth, which clinched the deal.

We were staying at **Tolon** (Τολόν), a pleasant, well-appointed resort close to the charming little fortress town of **Nafplion** (Ναύπλιον) in the Arcadian region of the **Peloponnese**. For a brief period this was the capital of modern Greece until Athens resumed her role. During our first week we had visited the

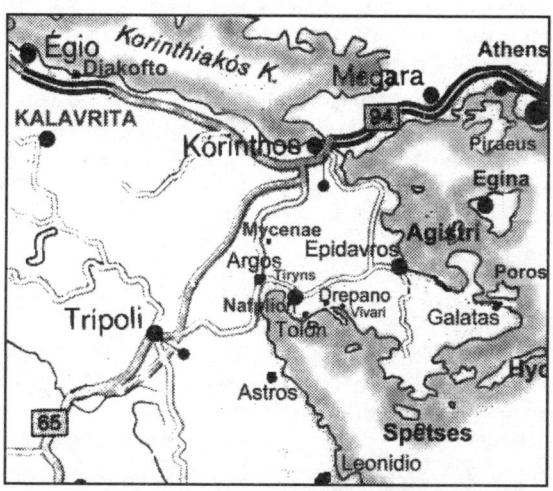

superb ancient amphitheatre at **Epidavros** (Επίδαυρος), we had climbed the hill through the Lion Gate of fabulous **Mycenae** (Μυκήναι) and had wondered at the Cyclopean walls of ruined **Tiryns** (Τύρυνς). So richly endowed is this north east corner of the Peloponnese with sites of historic and mythological interest that the ruins of legendary **Assini** (Ασίνη) that had sent two galleys of fighting men to besiege Troy, overlooked the beach we used at **Drepano** (Δρέπανο), unsigned and unexcavated.

Although it is warm in Greece in May, the countryside is fresh and green and the profusion of wild flowers in the fields and verges is remarkable for anyone more familiar with the sunburned browns of high summer and the end of the season. Vivid drifts of scarlet poppies were to prove a portent of our day.

As we approached our lunchtime stop at the upper rail terminus of **Kalavrita**, our courier, Eleni, who had been entertaining us with songs and stories explained that the town we were to visit had played a very special part in the history of modern Greece.

Fiercely proud of their Independent traditions the partisans of this district proved particularly uncooperative to the occupying German forces during the Second World War.

In the afternoon of an overcast day in December 1943, the entire male population of Kalavrita, 1,463 men and boys of twelve or more, were herded into the schoolyard and at 2.34 pm they were machine-gunned down in a grim reprisal. The town was torched. The nearby monastery of **Aghia Lavra**, previously a focus of resistance in the War of Independence of 1820 against the Turks, was also razed and the monks executed.

We drew into a small glade above the town where the massacre victims were buried. It was a shady spot surrounded by tall cedars and dominated by an immense azure and white Greek flag and a large white cross. In this idyllic place, loud with birdsong and the humming of bees, we examined the memorial plaques with the chilling repetition of family names found in any small rural community and the stark horror of lost young lives, conveyed by the dates carved in the cool marble. A simple modern sculpture marks the event.

Kalavrita is a bustling market town, renowned in Greece for its speciality rose petal jam. For years after the war, according to Eleni, it was a town of women dressed in mourning black. The old town was quickly rebuilt, as was the monastery up the hill.

After a leisurely lunch, alfresco in the Greek style, under the shade of plane trees in the town square, we moved on to visit the monastery, approached by a switchback road spectacular even by Greek standards. This is a place of pilgrimage for Greeks because of its national significance and that day its environs were mobbed. In the dark interior of the restored Byzantine nave with its burnished icons and the heady smell of incense we felt as if we were intruding on some very personal, though very public, grief as the crowds of pilgrims made their observances. We withdrew to the sunlit courtyard, silent with our thoughts, until our coach was ready to leave. Back at Kalavrita, Eleni pointed out the clock on the tower of the church. It was stopped at 2.34.

The rail trip, sweeping down to **Diakofto** through the **Vouraikos Gorge** (Φαράγγι Βουραϊκού), was every bit as exhilarating as we were told it would be. The two narrow gauge coaches are powered by a diesel unit placed between them. The original 1892 steam engine, impressively parked at the railhead, is long retired from duty.

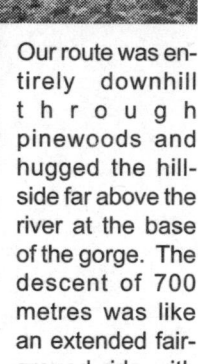

Our route was entirely downhill through pinewoods and hugged the hillside far above the river at the base of the gorge. The descent of 700 metres was like an extended fairground ride with much yawing, juddering and squealing of brakes and loud *"Oohs"* and *"Aahs"* as we swept over ravines on flimsy looking bridges and emerged from tunnels into sunlight.

A tiny station halfway down, at **Zachlorou** (Ζαχλωρού), serves the monastery of **Mega Spileo** (Μέγα Σπηλαίο), which could just be seen across the gorge, tucked under the lip of a precipitous cliff. Our rush to the coast continued and, down by the sea, we were able to swim in the Gulf of Corinth before meeting up with our coach and heading back to our resort and a late dinner.

I have many fond memories from my frequent visits to Greece, of the land and of the people, but my abiding memory is of that sun-dappled glade above Kalavrita.

Kythira Profile *by Andrew Mullett*

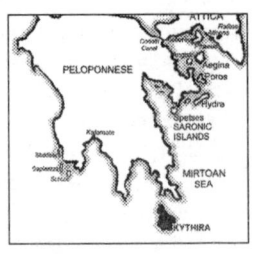

Kythira (Κύθηρα), sometimes spelt Kythera and by the airlines Kithira, is off the southern tip of the Peloponnese. It is 25 miles long and about 20 miles wide. Grouped with the Ionian Islands, Kythira lies apart from the others and is now administered from Attica.

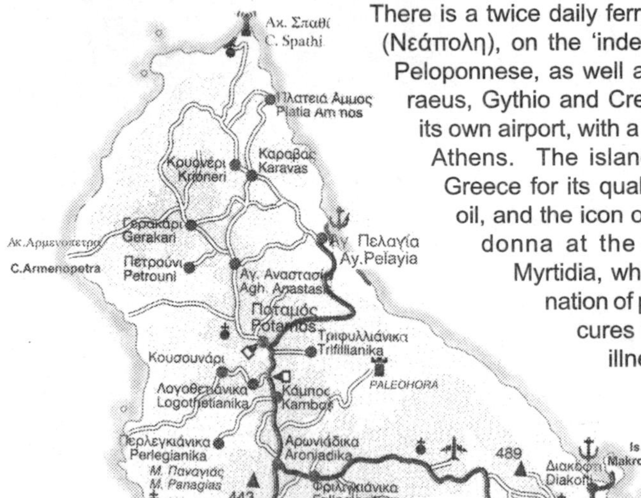

There is a twice daily ferry from **Neapoli** (Νεάπολη), on the 'index finger' of the Peloponnese, as well as links with Piraeus, Gythio and Crete. It also has its own airport, with a daily flight from Athens. The island is famous in Greece for its quality honey, olive oil, and the icon of the Black Madonna at the monastery of Myrtidia, which is the destination of pilgrims seeking cures for a variety of illnesses.

Since it remains off the main tourist routes

Kythira is quiet and very Greek, which is ideal for anyone interested in Greek culture - not the romantic sort with donkeys and little old ladies in black, but a work-

Adapted from Road Editions Peloponnese Map. Kythira map available

Gazing over Diakofti

ing, rural society. The main resort is **Kapsali** (Καψάλι) in the extreme south with unique double bays, a beach which is sandy at one end, and offers safe bathing in clear blue waters. It has bars, tavernas and places to stay. You can also stay in the nearby island capital **Hora** (Χώρα), also called Kythira Town, an exquisite white-painted village looking down on Kapsali from the top of high cliffs. It has banks and a post office as well as an impressive Venetian castle. Other resorts with rooms include **Ayia Pelayia** (Αγ.Πελαγία) in the north, which has four beaches close by, **Diakofti** (Διακόφτι) with its white sand beach, and the exquisite **Avlemonas** (Αβλέμονας) which has a famous fish taverna and a rocky cove reputedly frequented by Aphrodite. Close by is the 2km sandy beach of **Paleopoli** (Π.Παλαιόπολη). There are beautiful coves around the coast, all with pebble beaches, such as **Melidoni** (in SW), **Halkos** (SE) and **Kaladi** (E).

The ruined Byzantine citadel of **Paleohora** (Παλαιοχώρα) is a site of historic interest to visit, dramatically placed between forbidding cliffs. **Milopotamos** (Μυλοπόταμος) boasts a Venetian castle, a waterfall and a traditional kafeneion where you can sit all day under plane trees without being troubled. The interior has contrasting scenery, from fertile valleys full of olive groves to bare, dry uplands and deep gorges with running water. This makes the island a good destination for walkers and artists.

Kythira Background

❑ *The island has always had strategic importance because it stands at the gateway to the eastern Mediterranean. The Phoenicians and Minoans used it as a trading post, and established the city of Skandia on its eastern coast at present-day Paleopoli.*

❑ *The ancient Greeks believed the island to have been the birthplace of* **Aphrodite** *and built a temple to the goddess here. Menelaeus, King of Sparta, is said to have had a castle here, and his wife Helen served as a priestess in the temple. According to island legend, it was here that she was seen by Paris, who then carried her off to Troy.*

❑ *In Roman times the island was called* **Porphyrousa** *because it was the source of the seashell that yields the purple Porphyra dye used to colour the robes of the rich.*

❏ When the Roman empire broke up it came under the sway of Byzantium, but was then given as a marriage gift to the Venetians, who ruled it from the 13th until the end of the 18th Century. During the Napoleonic wars it became a British protectorate until it was given back to Greece in 1864. The island is littered with the fortifications of these conquerors.

❏ Lord Elgin pulled in at the port of Avlemonas, with marbles from the Parthenon. During a storm, one of his ships sank in the harbour and it took two years to raise the valuable relics and bring them to Britain.

Kythira: Land of Milk and Honey? *by Andrew Mullett*

Famed in classical times as the birthplace of Aphrodite, the Greek island of Kythira became in the eighteenth century a favourite subject for writers and painters of northern Europe. Notably Watteau, whose painting 'Embarkation for the Island of Cythere' is arguably one of the ten best ever painted. Yet Watteau and artists like him never visited the island. Their vision of a land of milk and honey was based entirely on tradition.

The sad fact was that life was hard on Kythira in the eighteenth century. Ruled by the Venetians since the 1200s only the noble rulers had any standard of living to speak of. The rest were poor peasants forced to give service to their Venetian masters and grow wheat on entirely unsuitable land for the granaries of Venice. Their diet consisted largely of the split pea porridge 'fava', eaten for breakfast, lunch and dinner.

Not until the imperialist British took over in the early 19th century was any serious attempt made to develop the island. They built roads and schools under a system of community service in which the islanders, peasants and reluctant Venetian nobles alike, were expected to give one day's labour a month. They even introduced what we know today as typical Greek food. The story goes that the British governor took receipt of a consignment of potatoes for planting, but the locals viewed the new food with suspicion and would not touch them. The governor promptly had them stored in a barn and issued a proclamation that they were extremely valuable and not to be taken away. The potatoes disappeared overnight. Through these efforts and the efforts of the locals themselves, after the British gave the island back to the emerging independent Greece in 1864, the island began to see some prosperity, evidenced by the presence of a number of large 19th century churches on the island.

However, these efforts collapsed after the bulk of the population debunked to Australia during the 20th century, the permanent population falling from a healthy 14,000 to the minuscule 3,000 it is today, leaving the island dotted throughout with ruined houses. The economy fell into the doldrums until very recently, when there has been some renewed interest in the island, helped by development grants from the European Community.

To the modern visitor, Kythira presents a vision of a modern Arcadia very similar to that of 18th century painters. You are free to wander among ruins aplenty, from abandoned houses to Venetian castles, even a German look-out post from the second world war, gently decaying among the wild flowers on its bleak headland above the sea. The difference is that the ruined houses present rich pickings for those with a lump sum looking for a site with potential or a retreat away from the stresses of the modern world: bucolic landscapes and sea views are not in short supply. Simply select your ruin and cough up the readies. Already some headway has been made in restoring the island's housing stock, as well as bringing much-needed building work to the island.

In my own role as a walks leader I have taken groups through landscapes of amazing beauty and emptiness. Tourism is very much in its infancy here, and what there is tends to be for the enthusiast, either for Greece, its culture and language, or for its hills and gorges as walkers, writers and paint-

Not far from Milopotamos

ers. Today's invaders come not to destroy, but to enjoy, including modern Athenians and returning Greek-Australians who have lost touch with their heritage and are seeking to regain it.

When walking through the landscape in autumn one can stop at an abandoned farm and feast on bunches of grapes half a metre long, growing among the weeds. Ripe figs drip from wayside trees and red strawberries hide among the foliage of the strawberry trees, sweet and succulent.

On top of this, local entrepreneurs have revived local products - olive oil, jams, wine, cheese and live yoghurt for instance, all of it organic for the simple reason that fertilisers have never made it to the island. Because of the nature of the land and the small scale of everything, methods are still largely traditional. The most famous product of all is Kythiran honey, bursting with flavour because of the abundance of thyme growing on the hillsides.

In the tavernas delicious meals of wild goat stifado are served up, as well as, in season, wonderful artichokes in lemon sauce. Because Kythirans love their vegetables, vegetarians can feast on a wide range of dishes throughout the season. Do not expect haute cuisine here, but rustic home cooking at its best with the freshest of ingredients, made on the day.

For those prepared to fork out the extra to get to a more distant destination, and to take the extra trouble of changing planes at Athens, Kythira is now truly a land of milk and honey and something of a paradise away from it all, but in a truer way than it has ever been before. It is an island which remains essentially Greek, but in a way which defies the myths and sentimentality that has dogged the image of Greece for too long.

A word of warning, though. The island, which is far to the south, off the end of the Peloponnese, is extremely hot in high season and full to capacity - not with overseas tourists, but with Greeks being noisy and very Greek. To appreciate the island at its peaceful best it is better to come slightly off season. With this reservation, it is an island to truly admire and return to over and over again - as indeed I do.

Avlemonas

How to get to Kythira
By Air - scheduled flights from Athens
By Ferry - from Neapoli, Kalamata, Gythion (Peloponnese) plus Antikythira, Chania (Crete), Piraeus.
Tour Operators - Explore Worldwide, Filoxenia, Freedom of Greece, Greek Tourism-Travel, Island Wandering

Rhodes, Island of the Sun God *by Paul Stickler*

We first arrived in Rhodes (or Rodos as it is called in Greece) some 15 years ago, on our first holiday abroad. My wife and myself, our friends and our young lads had decided to invest in a package holiday. We chose Rhodes because it, allegedly, had the best sunshine in the Med.

When we arrived at our Rhodes Town hotel in the early hours of the morning we had a bit of a culture shock! After manhandling the luggage up the endless flights of stairs to the rooms, (we'd brought enough clothes to last six months) and my bladder close to the point of no return, my first port of call was the bathroom. Very basic, I thought, but very clean also ... but what was the bin beside the toilet for? When I'd finished doing what I had to do, I decided to go downstairs and ask, and whilst I was there, I could replenish my bladder. I introduced myself to the barman, Kostas, who introduced me to Retsina, and after about four glasses of the firewater, I remembered why I'd come downstairs in the first place. When I asked Kostas what the bin was for

From Ancient Medieval & Modern Rhodes Guidebook published by GRECOcard Ltd

he laughed and poured me another Retsina. In his typically forthright manner, he explained about the small bore waste pipes used on the older properties in Greece, and the effect of throwing paper down the toilet. Feeling exceptionally stupid, I declined another drink and slipped back up to my room. That short time spent talking to Kostas, now known to us as 'The Oracle' was the beginning of my love affair with Greece, Rhodes in particular.

That two weeks holiday with our teenage sons was the best holiday we had ever had, up until then that is. The four of us adults have been going back to Rhodes each year, sometimes twice, ever since. The boys have now left home, have families and do their own thing, but they too have found themselves back on the island of the sun god, albeit without their parents.

We were typical British tourists in the first days. On our first visit to the beach we all duly rolled out our towels on the sand to do a bit of sun worshipping, unaware of the ferocity of the sun. We managed about half an hour before we fried and decided to grab a couple of sun beds and parasols, but the damage had been done. After getting back to the hotel, and taking several cold showers to momentarily ease the pain, we trudged downstairs to the bar looking like well done lobsters. Of course, Kostas and the other barman Nikos, fell about laughing and muttering 'crazy tourists' but when they had finished ridiculing us, they told us the best pain reliever for sunburn is yoghurt. We duly popped across to the supermarket and bought several gallons of the stuff, which did the trick for us. We have since taken care not to overdo it - medium rare being the order of the day.

Every year we return to the same hotel. The staff are now our very good friends and invite us to eat with their families at home on every available occasion. We, in turn, take out loads of presents when we visit. We even telephone Kostas, Eleftheria, Nikos and Katina every month or so to see how things are on 'Our Island' and they phone us on New Year's Eve to wish us a happy new year. How we all wish we could live there permanently.

As we became regulars, Mimis, the hotel owner, suggested we would be better off financially organising the hotel rooms privately and booking flights only rather than package tours. He was right! He saved us £800 a year, and for the privilege of booking privately, we took home a large bottle of Metaxa each, every year, courtesy of Mimis. He also brought us melons, grapes and nectarines from his other hotel (which he keeps solely for the Germans *"so there won't be any argument over sun beds"*) and Kostas brings us tomatoes, peppers, onions and fresh bread from his home *"to make sure you don't go hungry"*.

It was Kostas that recommended we try a little restaurant owned by Pavlos. It was situated down an alley and took us an age to find, but boy, are we glad we found it! As soon as we walked through the door Pavlos welcomed us and ushered us to the top table right in front of the air conditioning unit which he duly switched on. It was welcome relief, as it was early September and very warm, even at 8.30 pm. He came to sit by us with the menu and notepad and explained what was in each and every dish. He even gave us a couple of mezes free of charge. The lads had marinated octopus and the girls had tzatziki. In all honesty, we were very dubious at first about octopus, but have now become addicted to the stuff and have some whenever we can. The girls, however, still wrinkle up their noses when we do, and prefer to stick to good old tzatziki.

Pavlos also has now become a very good friend, and provided we give him 24 hours notice, will obtain and prepare anything we want - and I mean anything. His food is probably the best I've ever tasted.

Ippoton (Knights' Street)

I could probably write pages upon pages on places to go and things that have happened to us in Rhodes over the years - driving on the 'wrong' side of the road for example - and how unbelievably friendly the people are. There are so many memories, so much I could say. Over the past few years, Rhodes has had some bad press, due mostly to a few mindless idiots that have no respect for traditions and values. It is centred in one particular resort on the island, so we make a point of bypassing Faliraki, and we have had no problems whatsoever in 15 years.

Suffice to say we will be returning, hopefully for the next 15 years and more. We now regard it as home and feel safer there than in Britain. Who knows, maybe we'll win the lottery one day and retire there. Sure we have been to other Greek islands. They are all very beautiful, but we get drawn back every year to our friends and 'our island' - Rhodes, the island of the sun god, Helios.

A profile and traveller's notes on the Island of Naxos were featured in an earlier Greek-o-File publication, but Arthur Deeks' inimitable style of writing about his holidays with Harry have so much more to offer than just information. We make no apology for repeating a feature on the island of Naxos.

Last of the Summer Retsina - The Long Walk

by Arthur Deeks

The bus had dropped us conveniently close to **Ano Sangri** (Άνω Σαγκρί) and the solitary German who alighted before us confirmed the return departure point with the driver. Off he strode, purposefully, up the road. We stood looking at the deserted monastery of Agios Elefterios, having given only a cursory glance at the guide book. Suddenly out of the bushes came an old chap astride his donkey. He seemed trustworthy enough, jovial and full of bucolic charm - that was our third mistake. (*"No enemy is worse than bad advice"* - Sophocles, *Electra*)

"Kalimera"

"Kalimera sas. Engleesh?"

"Nai"

"Scotland?"

"Oxi - England"

"Temple?"

"Nai"

Diane Fryer

"Ekei" indicating left down the track from whence he had emerged *"eikosi lepta."* (20 minutes). *"Ekei..."* indicating the fast disappearing German *"mia ora"* (one hour).

And off he clopped.

Well that seemed to bear out the guide book, so off we stumbled down the track. An hour later and in the middle of a field of thorns, with scratched legs, surrounded by cacti, stone walls, impenetrable wire and deep gullies, I began to wonder about the post Iraq War graffiti we had seen in Naxos Town and a mountain village - *"F... Off Yanks and Brits"*. I had paranoid visions of the old Greek sitting in the local kafeneion, sipping his kafedakia, *"Guess what Yianni - I've just sent two ancient Brits down the old goat track, the one that goes to the thistle field. Beats writing graffiti on walls, eh Yianni?"*

Harry consulted his answer to a Global Positioning System - a minute compass which I suspect he got out of a Christmas cracker - and pronounced in true Nelsonian manner *"We're definitely going in the right direction."*

"We're not going anywhere" I sulked *"Let's go back to where we started."*

We retraced our steps, eventually found the track described by the guide book and came upon the attractive and partially reconstructed (which helps my limited imagination) **Temple of Demeter** - which was undoubtedly worth the pain.

We took the long way back to the bus stop, just in time for the midday bus, we thought. So did the, by now, very unhappy and agitated German whose ferry was due to leave in an hour. We waited, the poor man anxiously staring up the road. *"I could cheer him up by telling him some of my war stories"* said Harry quietly - *"No!"* I hissed, and eventually he fled towards Naxos town while we stoically waited, and waited, and waited - but eventually even our patience was exhausted. This had been our second mistake - believing the bus timetable and the bus driver. (*"Never trust KTEL bus drivers"* - Stavros Sophocles *Electra Kafeneion*).

We tried looking for sustenance, but alas no taverna, no kafeneion, so we were down to half a bottle of tepid water and two Werthers Originals. From his pocket Harry produced two matchbox size containers of raisins, *"There!"* he said triumphantly, *"Royal Naval survival training - did I ever tell you about the time I was adrift in an open boat..."* Harry gets more and more like Grandad in Only Fools and Horses.

We set off in the afternoon sun, walking for what seemed like hours down what had to be the quietest road in the whole of Greece until eventually we collapsed disconsolately on a grass verge. A car sped past and Harry raised a trembling thumb - but the driver just waved. Then an old pick-up truck came into view. Harry thumbed again and I put on my best 'near death' look and, miracles, faith in human nature was restored when the wonderful Petros stopped to pick us up. We all squeezed uncomfortably onto the front seat

Diane Fryer

and I engaged him in animated conversation for at least two minutes. Petros is 28, single, fits doors and windows and doesn't speak English. I told him we were British, retired, tired and hot. The conversation then subsided into an uncomfortable silence, we put on our 'smiley and most grateful' expressions and I silently vowed to redouble my efforts to learn more Greek. (No wonder they want us to ... off, we are so boring!)

In Naxos Town we fell out of the pick-up, with excessive expressions of gratitude to Petros, and into the nearest bar, nursing our tired and scratched legs. We ordered our Mythos and opened our almost unused guide book 'Naxos and the Small Cyclades - 30 walks on five islands' by Christian Ucke. Not reading it carefully *before* setting out had been our first mistake. We now noted '*Long trousers* are an advantage and there are *no tavernas* en route.' and most importantly '*Sometimes* the bus stops nearer the houses'!

The sea crossing from Mykonos via Paros had been pretty calm and uneventful and even the compulsory revisiting of Harry's sea stories were almost bearable. It also gave us the opportunity to plan the week and allocate responsibilities.

This year we decided, in line with current best management practice, to regularise our travel organisation. Harry was appointed Director of Domestic Affairs (mends equipment, makes tea, prepares wholesome breakfasts, washes up, dries the tea bags, etc). I was to be Director of Financial Services (keep the communal purse and if possible arrange for a 'divi' at the end.) We hadn't quite planned for this year's accommodation which was clean, well appointed and 'cosy' (a euphemism for 'Lilliputian'). In practice this meant the large and unconnected telephone was on the draining board; to use the kitchen area one either had to clamber over or move the beds; the balcony space was vital to allow movement around the room. No water shortage though, which eliminated the need for Harry to take one of his 'destroyer' baths. These are not as you may imagine, Harry thrashing about damaging fixtures and fittings, but the sort of ablutions necessitated by the cramped accommodation of an RN Destroyer - all this to the accompaniment of 'A Life on the Ocean Wave' (I made the last bit up - he can't sing!)

I first visited Naxos 25 years ago on a walking holiday, but found it hard to recognise much of it. It really has developed since then, but it remains delightful. Sure there are plenty of commercialised bits, a plethora of banks

and it probably teems with tourists at the height of the season - but it also has great charm and history.

Naxos, albeit a 'one town' island is the largest of the Cyclades and quite beautiful, with mountains - **Mt Zas** (Ορ.Ζας) is 1000 metres - lovely mountain villages, fertile valleys and the town itself has to be one of the most attractive in the Cyclades with its huge distinctive marble 'Portal' (Πορταρα) to the never-completed temple to Apollo on the islet of **Palatia** and the lovely old town and kastro. We were captivated by the maze of narrow alleyways which wind under archways, projecting stairs, overhanging balconies and which often end in a frustrating cul de sac, but sometimes reward with colourful cameos and vistas.

The long Venetian occupation 13th to 16th centuries shows not least in the unmemorable Catholic Cathedral and the excellent Domus Della Rocca-Barozzi Venetian Museum where apparently they have really good wine tasting sessions, *hic*, although we didn't go, honest.

I did remember the **Archaeological Museum** with its rare collection of early Cycladic figures (very defensive, all that folded arm stuff) and the roof terrace with the Hellenistic mosaic in pretty good condition, but not the **Mitropolis Museum** near the Grotta district because it wasn't open until

1999. One positive thing about visiting early in the season is that museums are pretty empty and you only have to interrupt the staff card games to get a ticket. On the down side, s o m e places didn't seem to be open, or saw us coming. One day we walked to the **Iria temple** which sounded interesting, but it was locked. I'm sure the exercise was good for us though.

Map adapted from
Efstathiadis Road Atlas

We considered hiring a car but they had had heavy winter rains and we heard some island roads, which aren't the best anyway, had been washed away or damaged. So we took the 'Island Coach Tour' which really was very good, with an excellent quadrilingual and highly informative guide. The down side of organised tours is that they get a bit kaleidoscopic and afterwards it is difficult to separate images and information. The tour included

Galanado (Γαλανάδο), with its interesting double chapel Greek Orthodox on one side, Roman Catholic the other, joined (or separated) by an arch - apparently there are others on Naxos - a symbol of ecumenicism or more likely a testimony to the tolerance of the former Venetian rulers. Also **Halki** (Χαλκεί) with its old Vallindras distillery where they used to prepare the delicious and quite high octane Naxos Citron liqueur distilled from unique citron tree leaves by a secret recipe.

A detour to **Moni** (Μονή) and the 6th century monastery of Panagia Drossiani constructed of grey stone, beautifully situated among olive trees, and with very interesting frescoes. On to **Filoti** (Φιλότι), the largest village on the island, **Apiranthos** (Απείρανθος), another peaceful little village and undoubtedly the most attractive we saw, paved with marble dominated by Venetian fortified dwellings it also has museums including an archaeological museum - the only one we found open. Finally on to **Apollonas** (Απόλλωνας) for lunch, a quick swim and a quick visit to the 10 metre long marble *kouros* abandoned as flawed in 6th century BC. It's a bit stark, difficult to see what it would have been like if erected - presumably it would have had folded arms like the other cycladic figures we saw - and it seemed to have shrunk since I first saw it.

After lunch Harry was having a postprandial snooze on a small bench when he was joined by three ample German ladies from our coach. As they eased

Diane Fryer

themselves into the vacant space he gradually shifted along and eventually toppled off the other end and walked away muttering *"lebensraum"* under his breath in his best Basil Fawlty manner.

The journey was along winding country roads, through beautiful mountainous countryside, returning via a particularly attractive coast road (west), way above the sea for most of the way, through peaceful unpopulated countryside with occasional spectacular sea views and the occasional track leading down to sea.

On balance Naxos offered one of the best selections of eating places hitherto encountered, all of which were acceptable and some superb. Sirocco

in the main square was excellent, but if it's full the Platia opposite is a very good alternative and pretty universally recommended. Vassilli in Old Market Street, with an agricultural decor, was excellent if pricey. Almost opposite Lucullus had some very interesting dishes 'Tomatoes in Pregnancy', 'Great Grandmother Angela's Meat Balls' and for cannibals the 'Pie of Aunty Mary'. Irini, nicely Greek and understated and Taverna Koutouki in a sort of alleyway also came recommended. At the latter we thought the view of the sky was excellent, the constant passage of lost souls with suitcases, interesting, and the 30 degree slope on the table, challenging. Harry (who sat sort of below me) said he hated to be talked down to and thought the place was going downhill fast.

Our preprandial occupation, while we sipped our medicinal ouzo on the waterfront, was watching the taverna staff hustling for their first customers. Obviously it is critical, particularly early season, because hardly anyone wants to be the first in any place. Harry and I feel we have identified a niche in the market which we could exploit to help pay for more Greek holidays. We could offer ourselves as 'early doors diners', ordering ostentatiously and then melting away to another assignment as soon as other customers arrive.

If you like to enjoy after dinner Jazz and Blues to go with your mints, the minute Lakridi, behind the town hall, is very cosy and pleasant, but like all such places is a bit pricey, so skill in carefully nursing drinks is important.

Naxos really does have a lot to offer and we agreed a week was not enough to do it justice. Lots to do and see, some really nice tavernas and one of the best bookshops I've found in the Aegean.

We will return - after we've done the rest of Greece!

Gavdos Profile *by Sylvia Cook*

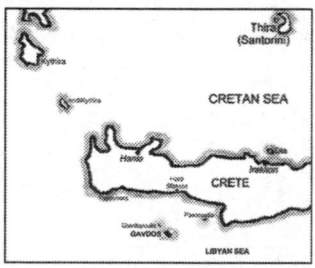

The tiny island of **Gavdos** (Γαύδος), lies in the Libyan Sea 50kms/22 miles roughly south of **Hora Sfakion** on the southwest coast of Crete and administratively under the jurisdiction of the Cretan Nomos of Hania. The island is just 10 kms long by 5 kms wide, roughly 30 sq kms. The southwest is rugged with a highest point of 384 metres. Mostly barren, the island has few springs and fertile areas. Its southern tip, **Tripiti** (Τρυπητή), is the southern most point of Europe.

Ferries arrive subject to weather conditions, from southwest Crete (Paleohora and Hora Sfakion), at the port of **Karave** (Καραβέ), where there are a few tavernas. **Ormos Sarakiniko** (Όρμ. Σαρακήνικο), the Bay of Saracens, has the best facilities for tourists and there is another small beach with taverna at **Korfos** (Κόρφος), plus beaches with no facilities at Tripiti, Ag. Ioannis, Potamos and Pirgos. The inland capital town of **Kastri** (Καστρί) is fairly deserted now, many of the population having left the island to seek prosperity elsewhere.

Gavdos Background

❑ *Settled in Neolithic times and called Ogygia in ancient times, the island is reputedly the mythical Island of the nymph Calypso who held Odyseus prisoner for some years. St Paul was said to have been blown past the island of Clauda, Gavdos' Roman name, before being shipwrecked. The Venetians called it Gotzo.*

❑ *It was certainly a populated island in Classical times, in the Middle Ages 8,000 reputedly lived on Gavdos, in 1914 about 1400, but today barely 40-70 people remain all year round.*

❑ *Today's few inhabitants are fishermen, sheep and goat farmers and summer taverna owners - in some cases all three.*

Gavdos, The Isle of Calypso *by Paul Burlison*

Gavdos is the legendary home of the nymph Calypso (Καλυψώ), who detained Odyseus as prisoner for six years during his epic journey after the battle at Troy. She even offered him immortality if he would stay there, but in spite of the wonderful life he enjoyed, his need to return to family and his homeland got the better of him and Calypso was persuaded by the gods to assist his departure. I personally can't think of a better place to be kept prisoner and can fully understand his sadness on leaving.

Having visited and lived on the island 8 times in 6 years, I feel I'm going home when I arrive, or leaving home when my trip ends. I have never met a more magnanimous group of people in my many years of travelling around Greece, than I have in Gavdos, even though with massive depopulation there are few families still living there.

The west coast is nothing but horrifying precipices, which, although dramatic from the sea are inaccessible by land. A few years ago a Greek girl had a very serious fall trying to scale these - a warning to others.

Sarakiniko, on the north coast has a beautiful shallow bay with a vast stretch of sand and sand dunes covered with small cedar and pine trees which make the natural aroma quite unforgettable and second to no other place I know. (If only I could capture and sell it in jars ... but there again, perhaps not!!)

Sarakiniko has a number of tavernas, in my opinion the best and most natural you will find anywhere. Forget your tourist tavernas with plastic covered menus, here you get fresh fish, goat meat, local wine and more at very reasonable prices in a setting which is priceless. The Ogygia (Homer's name for Gavdos) is a favourite of mine, with unique pillars painted in Minoan and classical styles. Its owner, Giorgos (also known as Mexicanos since he

The Ogygia

returned from travelling one time wearing a Mexican hat!) is not only an extremely good cook, but being ex-merchant navy has many amusing tales and a wicked, but lovable, sense of humour. At the other end of the beach towards **Turtle Rock** (so named because of its shape) are two more good tavernas owned by brothers Damboulis and Nikos. I challenge anyone to find a more genuine, rugged, humorous and handsome pair of Cretan shepherds. They are unique. There's never a dull moment in their company. The view from here is shown in glorious colour on the front cover of this book. The next taverna along is owned by a third brother Giorgos.

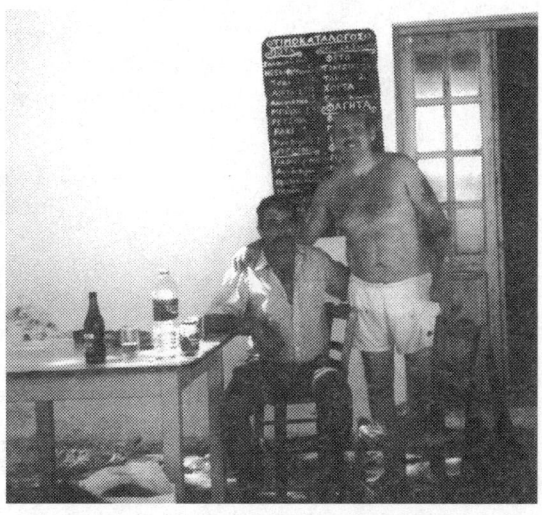

To help my friends (and to eke out my resources on longer trips) I've painted and varnished a few tavernas and created frescos of Odyseus' boat, dolphins and a sphinx, not to mention helping with a few blackboard menus (such as this one behind Damboulis and me in photograph).

You can rent rooms at several places, including Nikos' which I would personally highly recommend. His wooden taverna was the first in Sarakiniko and his food and rooms (all with WC and shower) are of a good standard as well as being ideally placed on the beach, 50-80 metres from the sea. He also sells Gavdos T-shirts. There is NOW a mini-market in Sarakiniko which has a good area for enjoying a drink or meal. A few years back there were very few provisions available on the island and I can remember days when the boat was delayed and visitors especially were craving for cigarette supplies. Every visitor should be aware of the weather conditions as stormy seas will often delay the boat for days, causing schedules to change. I've seen a fair number of people panicking about their connecting bus and flight home and a few do actually miss it. The situation amuses the locals, but I must say that they too pray for the boat to arrive.

In Greece's past history of dictatorial governments, Gavdos was used as a place of exile for political opponents. The taverna at the end of the bay

opposite Turtle Rock is that of the exiles. I could imagine them gazing out to distant Crete from here. The views are quite exceptional.

View across beach and sea to Crete from Nikos' Taverna

Korfos on the east coast is a much smaller shingle beach which had one taverna last time I was there.

The capital of the island is **Kastri**, but if you are expecting bright lights here, forget it. However it does have a police station, the doctor is here and a few locals hang on tenaciously in spite of the massive depopulation and deserted houses around them.

The other two inhabited villages on the island are **Vatsiana** (Βατσιανά) in the south east and **Ambelos** (Αμπέλος) in the south west linked by road to the capital. Vatsiana has the only museum on the island, which is certainly worth a visit, if only to see how the islanders lived here in the past. There is a kafeneion here serving the small number of inhabitants.

A recently built taverna before you get to **Ag. Ioannis** beach is home to an array of colourful characters who visit from Athens, Thessaloniki and other parts of Greece during the summer - all good fun for practising one's Greek. I've spent many a pleasant evening on its starlit benches by the 'camp' fire eating delicious sea urchins.

You can walk to **Tripiti** (Τρυπητή) from Vatsiana or from Korfos. It is an amazing place with just its natural beauty of cedars and pine trees behind a vast stretch of beach, with goats grazing on sea grasses. There is an old derelict house with a tree and seats to rest on the way from Vatsiana, but be warned, there is nowhere else for shelter and it can get extremely hot at this southern-most tip of Europe.

Gavdopoula (Γαυδοπουλα) is a little sister island to the north west of Gavdos. Not much more than a big rock really, but it does have one beautiful little cove which you may be able to hire a fisherman to take you to. I've heard locals, when asked by visitors where they can get something, reply *"Paleohora if you want everything or Gavdopoula for nothing, but Gavdos is paradise with or without"*.

In Gavdos there is no mains electricity, but this is not a problem as everything runs on personal generators. A few years ago, Stratis (who owns a few goats, a taverna, etc) had a new generator sent over from Sfakia on the boat. After winching this machine up, everyone was involved in gently guiding it over the keel to the quay at the main port of **Karave** (Καραβέ). Suddenly it broke from its ropes and fell, hitting Stratis. It honestly looked like it had killed him, but fortunately he survived after being escorted back onto the boat to Crete with the doctor, then to the hospital in Hania.

Karave has a small jetty and two small tavernas, one with rooms for rent and the other a true rustic taverna. Roula, the *'yiayia'* of the family is the sweetest, funniest and sharpest old lady you could ever wish to meet. She is truly wonderful and it is always such a pleasure to see her wave to us as we arrive, but rather sad yet fortifying when she waves you off. One time

Roula and Enza

we offered her some locust beans we'd bought in Crete - she very quickly pointed out to us that she had no teeth! She gave Enza and I a hand made lace mat which lies affectionately on our modern TV in England and constantly reminds us that they are all waiting in paradise for us to return.

It is interesting to see the changes in the Gavdos people over the years. There is one lad I always look forward to seeing, the son of another good friend of mine. I first knew him as a 14 year-old driving his father's tractor, tending the goats and helping with the daily chores of running an island taverna. I watched him grow rapidly over the years and he's grown into a smashing young man. It's quite amusing seeing the girls chase after him; his father rightfully is very proud of him. Two years ago it was his time to do military service. After 2 weeks he ran away from Athens and returned to Gavdos. The island policeman had been ordered to find him and send him back on the next boat, but he told him he had a week to get himself prepared, then he must return. Meanwhile the policeman reported back that he could not find him, but inevitably would in the foreseeable future. The lad dutifully returned. I saw him briefly on a flying visit, but it will be interesting to see how city and military life has affected him when we return.

In the years I've been going to Gavdos I've seen it slowly develop, no mass tourism (thank God), but a few new tavernas have appeared and a new road has been made from the port of Karave to Sarakiniko.

The number of visitors seems to increase each year, so when, as inevitably they will, more people do go to Gavdos, it would be nice to think that Greek-o-File readers who visit are the more discerning respectful kind who like the unspoilt islands as they are. I spoke to several Gavdos locals about writing this article as most are against major developments, but they are a friendly bunch and wholeheartedly agreed that exposure in the 'right' places, brings the most welcome kind of visitors. They look forward to meeting you and sharing their island paradise.

How to get to Gavdos

By Air - to Crete (Hania is best) then bus to Hora Sfakion or Paleohora on the south coast

Then by Ferry - variable weekdays from Paleohora (3.5-4 hrs) or Fri, Sat & Sun from Hora Sfakion (3 hrs) to Karave

Tour Operators - NONE known at present. You can pre-book accommodation at some travel agencies in Paleohora, or with some UK 'tailored holidays' companies.

Our Charioteer *by Judith Hepper*

We were all a little anxious. *"The coach will leave at three"*, we had been told, and, though 'relaxed' and 'independent' were the key words on this tour, we had learnt to take pride in scrambling onto our shining green-and-gold chariot *on time*. But now, where was our charioteer?

We were also a little shocked. Hitherto we had wandered the Peloponnese unhindered, as if it were the very dawn of civilization, arriving at sites still fresh and cool in the early-morning light and exploring them almost in solitude. But now we had joined the tourist trail - quiet though it was in mid-October - at Olympia. True, we had found a shady spot high on a hill above the stadium, where we could enjoy our picnic among the wild cyclamen, but we had been faced with postcard racks, food-stalls, school parties and strident warning whistles for the first time. We huddled together, caught for a moment between rows of coaches, engines revving, drivers shouting, finding themselves more helplessly jammed by the minute. Suddenly, a cheer went up! Down the road that skirted the dusty car-park drove our charioteer, for all the world like a god descending from Mount Olympus! Had he been washing his coach, with water from some Arcadian spring? Or dallying with the wood-nymphs in a nearby olive grove? Unquestioningly, we jumped aboard and were whisked away, our round of applause for Christos received with an aloof smile.

Christos has been the coach-driver for 'Damaris' for many years. Dark-haired, stocky, attentive but never effusive, he was imperturbable and utterly indispensable. He appeared each day in a clean white shirt and in freshly-polished shoes, a contrast to our comfortable, casual outfits. The only time we saw Christos less than unruffled was at Nemea. A short shower of rain, and our own curiosity, meant that when we returned to the coach our sandals and trainers were caked with the glutinous yellow clay of the stadium and the hills above. Wordlessly, Christos lined us all up and hosed

down our feet, on full nozzle, relentlessly, until he was satisfied that not a clod remained. A little damp, but with some hilarity, we tiptoed on board. Occurring on Day One (of eight), the 'Washing of the Feet', as it became known, turned out to be the perfect icebreaker.

Christos, however, was impervious to our moods, and to our various passions: butterflies, wild flowers, sketching, photography, transcribing Linear B and studying O.U. texts among them. There was only one exception: miraculously, the coach would be stopped if Jane (our tour leader) exclaimed with interest at wayside plants. Christos would leap off to pluck sweet chestnuts, cotton fluff and even prickly pears for her delight. And on the coast, at Methoni, Christos revealed a passion of his own. While we swam in the limpid Mediterranean as the sun set radiantly over the Venetian castle, Christos gravitated to a group of fishermen on the harbour wall and quickly had a rod in his hand, catching brightly-coloured fish with expert ease.

We all assume the Greeks to be orators and Christos lived up to our expectations. From his driver's seat he would engage in rapid and passionate declamation. An oracular voice? A rhetorician? No, no! The proud owner of a state-of-the-art mobile telephone! We benefited, of course, as Christos would frequently be ringing ahead to check on hotel-bookings, parking spaces or museum opening times. Those who elected to eat together at 'the best' (in Christos' well-informed view) local taverna that evening could have their tables booked and even their menus ordered.

Christos also enjoyed his conversations with Antonio, a young Spanish member of the party, in a mixture of European languages. But the liveliest conversations were with people we met on the road. Christos would lean from his high coach window to chat to olive harvesters, farmers (with their wives perched on the back of tractors or donkey carts) and the drivers of lorries full of chickens or oranges, checking the way to a new stretch of road, perhaps, or a little-visited archaeological site. There seemed to be all the time in the world to talk in the sun - and yet we were never late!

During our three days in Athens (Christos, a true Greek, has never been on to the Acropolis but he promises to come next year ...) we celebrated the seventeenth birthday of Mike, the youngest member of the party this year, and Christos' willing assistant in the Herculean task of heaving our luggage out of the bus's cavelike hold nearly every evening. Christos decided to entertain us at his favourite taverna, and there we had the time of our lives among his friends. The bouzouki players never had a break, small children clapped the rhythm, retsina flowed, older men put down their worry-beads and performed slow, curiously ritualistic dances, mezes multiplied, songs (clearly patriotic, subversive or suggestive in turn - how we longed to understand the language!) were sung in solo or unison, and Christos' own sixteen-year-old daughter enchanted us with her dancer's grace and skill.

At midnight a huge birthday cake was borne in, to be cut by Mike and shared with us all. And the unflappable Christos, he who edged his beloved coach round village streets so narrow that we missed brightly-painted shutters and potted hibiscus with only centimetres to spare, he who negotiated his passengers along the knife-edge precipices and jutting rock-faces of the Tayetos Mountains with breathtaking ease, suddenly threw all caution to the winds and danced with the abandon of a Maenad, feet kicking the air until he was completely horizontal, suspended only by the handkerchief held in his teeth. How we cheered!

Now our photographs hold the memories of this wonderful experience.

The beach at Methoni

One of my favourites (which only works in colour) shows four seated passengers reflected in the windscreen of Christos' coach. Freddy and John look wide-awake and full of anticipation. Intrepid, both in their eighties, a fund of good stories and wide-ranging knowledge, they are enthusiastic travellers. Perhaps they have just gasped at their first sight of the massively weighty masonry of the walls that climb up to the Lion Gate at ancient Mycenae, or caught a magical glimpse of the mist-wreathed Byzantine churches high above the mountain road at Mystra.

The younger pair are sleeping (quite right too - Susanna will be a mother for the first time in January, and sleep is precious just now). Maybe they are dreaming of the tiny early Psi figure of a mother feeding her baby which delighted us in the Museum at Nemea, or of the stroll along the beach to see the floodlit castle of Nafpaktos before our romantic supper at tables set out on the sand opposite our hotel. Perhaps they are simply tired after the long walk in the vale of Messene. Certainly they are lulled by the quiet comfort of Christos' coach and aware, as we all are, that faultless preparation, and the effortless travel from site to site which Christos ensured, have enabled us to make an unforgettable journey through ancient Greece.

Photographs by James Willis, who was on the same Damaris' Journey Through Ancient Greece (see p179 for details).

Profile of The Mani by Sylvia Cook

The **Mani** (Μάνι) region is most easily identified as the middle finger of the Southern Peloponnese. Split into **Inner** (Μέσα) or Deep Mani in the south and **Outer** (Έξω) **Mani** above backed by the **Taygetos** (Ταύγετος) Mountains, the tallest peak is Profitis Ilias, 2404m, the highest in the Peloponnese.

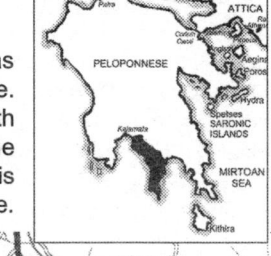

The north to south ridge naturally separates the administrative regions of Messinia (W) and Lakonia (E&S).

South east of **Kalamata**, Outer Mani is more accessible, more green with hillside villages, gorges, streams, dramatic mountains and more tourist resorts. **Stoupa** (Στούπα) was bound to become the busiest development with its beautiful wide sandy bay, but it still retains a certain charm. **Kardamyli** (Καρδαμύλη) has a more rugged coast and an old town with tower houses. **Ag Nikolaos** (Αγ. Νικόλαος) is a fishing village clustered around a harbour. Traditional and uniquely styled pale limestone buildings are obvious in Outer Mani, including many built recently. Inner Mani is more barren and whole villages of old stone tower houses, such as **Vathia** (Βάθεια) or **Kita** (Κοίτα),

Adapted from
Road Editions
All Greece Map.
Peloponnese
map available.

Byzantine churches and treeless hills dominate. There are no typical tourist resorts in the south although accommodation is available in and near most coastal villages. Try **Itilo** (Οίτυλο), **Areopoli** (Αρεόπολη), **Gerolimenas** (Γερολιμένας), **Porto Kayio** (Πόρτο Κάγιο) in the south, or **Gythio** (Γύθειο) on the northwest coast as bases to explore from.

Only rediscovered in 1958 the **Diros** Caves (Διρού) were first inhabited by Palaeolithic painters, but now you can be punted around in a boat to look at spectacular stalactite formations.

The Mani Background

❑ *Taygetos was named after Taygete, daughter of Atlas the giant. She was a shy and reluctant mistress of Zeus who gave birth to Lakedemon who later married Sparti to found the Spartan nation. Artemis helped Taygete avoid Zeus' attentions by turning her into a hind to hide from him in the mountains. In later millennia the mountains were to offer protection to the Maniots (descendants of the Spartans and a Slavic race).*

❑ *Kardamyli is the site of the tomb of the **Dioscouri**, heavenly twins Castor & Pollux, born to Leda after Zeus seduced her in the form of a swan. Leda was also the mother of Helen. **Kranai**, where Helen and Paris spent their first night together before going to Troy, is Homer's name for Marathonisi, the islet joined by a causeway to **Gythio**. **Cape Tenaro** (Ακ.Ταίναρο), the furthest point south on the Greek mainland, is another contender for the entrance to Hades.*

❑ *The Maniots resisted and delayed many historical changes forced on their northern neighbours. Even Christianity did not take a hold until many centuries after Byzantium was established and there were constant uprisings against Venetian and Turkish rulers.*

❑ *When not rebelling against their rulers, the violent Maniots were attacking each other. The legendary blood feuds are the reason for the distinctive stone tower architecture of the region. Men attacked and murdered the men of neighbouring families who had 'upset' them (often over trifling matters, maybe generations before) from their battle towers by their family homes. The towers were built ever higher to improve defence and attacking capabilities. Canons fired from roof to roof, guns, swords, knives, axes, anything was used for hand fighting. Women and priests (not targeted) delivered supplies. The last great feud ended in 1870 in Kita when troops were sent in to stop fighting.*

❑ *Truces were called at harvest time and occasionally for greater causes. Many families united in the rebellion led by Petrobey **Mavromichaelis** in March 1821, the first battle of The Greek War of Independence.*

Majestic or Manic Mani *by Sylvia Cook*

The Mani region had always fascinated me. We first intended to visit several years back on a return trip driving to Patra from Piraeus. We had five days, but hadn't quite appreciated the size of the Peloponnese so only managed to cut across the top of the 'fingers' that time. Our opportunity came in September 2003 whilst the last book was at the printers. We daren't pre-book anything at this time, but as soon as we knew all was safely in their hands we looked for an 'instant' break - avoiding the cheapest last minute holidays that do not specify more than your arrival airport. As Paul Stickler says in his article *"Rhodes has much to offer"*, but the chance of ending up in Faliraki didn't bear thinking about!

We struck lucky and found a week's holiday with Direct Greece flying to Kalamata on Sunday and staying in pleasant studios at the charming fishing village of **Ag. Nikolaos** just a few miles south of Stoupa. It was just the kind of place we would have chosen given more time to book.

The drive from **Kalamata** (Καλαμάτα) was quite spectacular. The forested Taygetos mountains loomed in front of us, then we turned south, zig-zagging into the hills and overlooking the Gulf of Messinia. We crossed a steep sided gorge on a modern (70s we were told) tarmac'ed road bridge from which we could see an old Venetian bridge far below and a German war built bridge half way up. The local architecture soon became apparent - inland villages with square towers obvious in the distance and many 'copy-cat' modern structures using traditional local stone along our route. We passed through **Kardamyli** and behind **Stoupa** on the main road before

Ag.Nikolaos, Mani

arriving at our destination. Our studio in **Ag. Nikolaos** was in a small block, just a 10 minute stroll away from the pretty harbour of this working fishing village - just perfect.

Our favourite spot that week was at a kafeneion where locals sat with their coffees and ouzos overlooking a long marble slab beside the harbour where the fishermen's multicoloured catches were displayed for sale. It was perfect for pre or postprandial drinks, for daytime coffees, or while waiting for the bus that stopped nearby. You could watch the fish being unloaded, weighed and displayed with great ceremony while the coffee drinkers passed comment from their ringside seats.

There was a more modern kafeneion with a large TV outside, a bar, souvlaki/gyros shop and about 3 more tavernas along the harbour front plus a couple more tavernas round the headland. The harbour road tavernas were best value with beers mostly at €1.50 and reasonably priced meals. A post office, pharmacy, two minimarkets and just a few tourist shops completed the facilities. Another bonus was sparkling clear local spring water freely available at several roadside taps in the village. With single rows of tables outside the harbour road tavernas and unusually mostly female waiting staff we found it took a few days to get talking to people - although the fishermen were more chatty at the harbour.

A 15 minute stroll along the waterfront past seaweed and eroded rocks lead to a pleasant sand and shingle beach with beach bar behind and a little further along a smaller beach overlooked by a welcoming shady taverna.

Ag Dimitrius was the next village along within strolling distance of the second beach, but although there was tourist accommodation, a tower and tiny harbour, there were no eating places. The whole area is ideal for walking inland too - up to the small village of **Ringlia** (Ρίγκλια) and on to **Eleochori** (Ελαιοχώρι) or further, depending how much energy you have.

Buses run regularly from **Itilo** (Οίτυλο) to **Kalamata** so the Outer Mani resorts were easily accessible. We took the bus to **Kardamyli** one morning (just 90 cents) to wander around. The main road cuts through the village with old buildings either side. A walk up to the old village brought us to the partly renovated tower houses and church of the ruling family in the 1800s.

This was our first battle tower seen up close, the only one we actually clambered around. It was here that Kolokotronis established his headquarters and entertained Mavromichaelis when he brought his Mesa Maniot troops marching to Kalamata to defeat the Turks in 1821.

The beaches (pebbly) are either side of the resort and accommodation mostly set in leafy side streets leading to cliff top views. A few tavernas overlooked the sea, but most activity seemed to be along the main road.

After an enjoyable lunch, we caught the bus back, getting off at **Stoupa** - THE tourist resort of the area. With its soft sandy beach in a sheltered

bay, and small harbour, backed by olive groves and mountains, I can imagine that it was *truly* idyllic once. Although much developed now, it attracts families, couples and many regulars. The tavernas we saw that afternoon and another evening were friendly and we saw no sign of noisy bars or discos. A not-to-be-missed speciality of the area is the 'pig-roast', ordered by the kilo, or for a number of people and delivered to your table carved in chunks and slices on an open sheet of butchers' paper for diners to tuck in. Quite delicious.

It took us less than an hour to walk back from Stoupa to Ag Nikolaos along the coastal pathway. A pleasant walk, not difficult to follow in September, but walk *round* the taverna half way if it appears closed - the gate at the other side was locked!

Perhaps because of the potentially long journeys to sites in the Peloponnese, car hire is expensive here, so we had a car just one day to explore Deep Mani to the south. The road to Itilo wound through villages with count-

less Byzantine churches and stone houses. Olive trees became more squat, fields more stoney as we headed south, with the early sun still behind the high mountain range. We were to see a marked difference between Exo and Mesa Mani terrain.

Itilo was a strategic town in ancient times, and capital of Mani until quite recently. It sits above the wide **Limeni bay**, from which pirates operated and slaves were traded in the 16th to 18th centuries. Today there is minimal coastal development from **Neo Itilo** to **Limeni** (Λιμένι)'s peaceful rocky edged harbour.

After the new capital town of **Areopoli** (Αρεόπολη), the town of Ares god of War, we headed eastwards to catch the morning sun - the opposite direction to most guidebook descriptions, but it worked for photography and the weather, as rain clouds gathered in the west and travelled east, between sunny spells. **Kotronas** (Κότρωνας) on the east coast had a few local shops and kafeneia along its main access road and 2 tavernas by the jetty jutting into the pebbled bay. New stone building was much in evidence. We stopped for coffee and some feta by the harbour before setting off down the east coast, stopping first at the small village of **Flomochori** (Φλομοχώρι) to wander round a few narrow streets behind the small plateia, looking at houses and war towers and trying to sense what life was like there not so long ago.

The roads were fairly deserted, the mountain ridge to the west known fittingly as Kakovounia - Bad Mountains - was barren, with villages of old stone houses and towers rising up behind the last olive trees and blending into the colour of the rock face behind. **Kokkala** (Κοκκάλα) on our road seemed a more modern development, but copying the style of the old stone towers, even with unfinished battlements to make them look like ruins! Maybe it was the black and grey clouds rolling across between the sunshine and blue skies, but we found it rather depressing that people should want to emulate these building details of the former warmongering inhabitants.

We took a chance on the 'white' road to **Marmari** (Μαρμάρι). Although the tarmac finished soon, the dirt road after was well flattened and from high up near **Korogonianika** (Κορογονιάνικα) we were rewarded with an incredible clear view down to the tip of the peninsular at **Cape Tenaro**, the beaches of **Porto Kayio** (Π.Κάγιο) east and **Marmari** west of the narrow strait and **Harakes Tower** in prime position between, overlooking the strait.

We started our return up the west coast. **Vathia** (Βάθεια) loomed on the left - a large cluster of war-towers, old and restored houses. It must have been a very dangerous place with so many feuding families living as close as that. From here there was a succession of villages with old and renovated tower houses clustered together. The fishing village of **Gerolimenas** (Γερολιμένας) was a more welcoming destination, although with much building work in progress, old stone and concrete buildings, white pebble beach and

Vathia

thunder clouds gathering again, it seemed more like an off season Cornish fishing village - and yet an ideal base for walkers and explorers. We found a 'Μεζεδοπολειου' offering a host of fresh meze dishes at reasonable prices.

The road north continued past more old stone villages. We took a parallel road inland to investigate further, finding villages mostly renovated, with olives, flowers in courtyards, many prickly pear cacti and generally more vegetation this side of the mountain. As we got further north the buildings were more utilitarian. All churches we attempted to explore were locked and we felt it was not worth trying to find the keyholder. We resisted the turning to the **Diros Caves** having heard there can be queues - but had we had the car another day would have liked to explore the caves and **Gythio** on the north east coast too, perhaps staying overnight in Mesa Mani.

All in all we would recommend The Mani, although we found it quite different from other parts of mainland Greece and the islands. Exo Mani in the north offers more hospitable surroundings, but Mesa Mani is certainly an unusual phenomenon and interesting to explore.

How to get to The Mani
By Air - scheduled via Athens to Kalamata, Charter direct to Kalamata
By Ferry - Gythio & Kalamata to/from Kythira & Chania (Crete),
Gythio to/from Pireaus
Tour Operators - Direct Greece, Filoxenia, First Choice,
Greek Options, Greek Tourism-Travel, Kosmar, Manos,
Olympic Holidays, Simply Travel, Simpson Travel, Sunvil.
Walking & Nature Holidays - ATG, Explore Worldwide,
Natural History Travel, Ramblers.

Inspired by Kardamyli *by John White*

Kardamyli (Καρδαμύλη) lies at the foot of the **Taygetos Mountains** (Op. Ταΰγετος), on the west coast of the Outer Mani and at the mouth of the **Viros** (Βιρός) Gorge. The older village hidden in the gorge, the church of St Spiridon (Αγ. Σπυρίδονος) and four old tower houses remain; some restored and inhabited, one a museum - but all seeming so peaceful that it's hard to imagine the feuds for which these miniature castles were built.

The modern village has a small harbour, a few stone houses and a good selection of tavernas, hotels and rooms to let.

The area is recommended for walkers, artists, writers and nature lovers. You don't have to be all of these, but as always, walkers see the best of the landscape. Kardamyli is the natural starting point for a network of well waymarked paths and maps are now available.

In the changeable weather when I was there in May, I didn't attempt the 2-3 day trek over the mountain range; the distances which I covered in one day walks were rather unimpressive. Even the steep ascents are eased by the skilfully engineered *kalderimia* (cobbled paths), which cling to slopes so abrupt that a metre wide path can require 4 metres or more of wall on the outer side.

The joy of this area, and the reason it kept me fully occupied for two weeks, is that it packs so many experiences into a short distance. Walking is less

an athletic achievement than an opportunity to notice, not only the distant peaks and the magnificence of the gorge, but also the wild flowers (which overgrow the paths so densely in places that I was advised to carry a stick to ward off adders), the swallowtail butterflies, the contortions of the olive trunks, the sites of waterfalls in the dry bed of the gorge, life in the villages ... it is so easy to be waylaid. I was drawn into seeking to understand, to explain, to join the writers and artists ... and to return late again to Kardamyli as the sun sinks behind the cape.

Next morning, if the sketch doesn't quite live up to the memory, the experience of acquiring both still seems worthwhile.

At each turning
Another wonder awaits me:
The oregano which scents the warm air and intoxicates
The breeze which now and then flickers silver
    through the olive trees and refreshes
The flank of the mountain which shows its white ribs
The cypresses in the gorge below, which hide sun-bleached tiles.
After a few paces, I make out the dome of a monastery
The black webs on the wings of the swallowtail butterflies
    which suck the thistles,
The austere beauty of a church built of sandstone, dark with age,
Isolated on the bare pale rocks, it insisted that I draw it carefully.
A lizard darts and freezes,
Poised to run
Its spine a curve
As if it was time which stopped
The very kalderimi which I tread so easily,
    so skilfully did the Maniots build it.
The next turning beckons me
Only
    because of the wonders
        do I dawdle.

Going Underground *by Peter Greaves*

Greek-o-File's Volume 2 article on climbing Mt Olympus reminded me of my exploit when I and two companions climbed that rock from Lithorio with an overnight at the hostel. It was October and moist. The cold clear night was minus 10°C so the moisture froze like glass onto the rock but the day's clear sky was sunny and melted this coating. The 'Bad Steps' is described in the guidebooks as 'airy'. I have to say it was *scary*, requiring a confident commitment to swing around the corner. The top was worthwhile and the return down the scree to the Zonaria path a pleasant scramble where it contoured round in bright sunshine above rising cloud.

But enough of these reminiscences. Not only do I go up - I go down.

Being from Derbyshire I had noticed that most of Greece is made of limestone like at home. And limestone forms caves where the water dissolves the limestone from cracks and joints and creates underground watercourses which enlarge the cavities. But the dissolved limestone in the supersaturated solutions can be deposited as stalagmites and/or stalactites if the water evaporates slightly. These natural formations have been exploited as tourist attractions in Derbyshire at Castleton and Matlock Bath. Despite my inherent chauvinism, the Derbyshire attractions are not a patch on those I have seen in Greece. There are over 3,000 caves in Greece, so it is appropriate to call cave exploration speleology (Greek *spelea* σπηλιά = cave), however only about 20 show-caves have organised tours that I know of.

My first Greek caves were the sea caves on the west coast of **Paxos** in the Ionian. They were relatively shallow indentations in the coast visited by boat under overhanging cliffs. Some of them had collapsed roofs and further erosion resulted in sea arches (Tripitos Arch) comparable to Durdle Door in Dorset and eventually to sea stacks (Orlithos). **Ipapanti** cave (on Paxos) was reputed to have hidden a Greek submarine in World War II between raids on Axis shipping.

My first serious caves were at **Diros**, 8 kms outside Areopolis in the **Mani**. There are four caves here and a museum of Neolithic finds. These caves were discovered in 1895 and explored in 1950 by the husband and wife team of Iannis and Anna Petrohilos. Vlihada cave, opened in 1963, is visited by boat along 2.5 km of channels with electric lighting to enhance the natural formations which are reflected in the water. The adjacent Alepotrypa cave has evidence of use as a Neolithic shelter (5300BC). Katafigi and Glyfada caves complete the group and it is suggested that this is part of a complex extending north under the Taygetos massif for 60 km to Sparta.

Five km **north of Ioanina** in Epirus is the cave of **Permaga**. This was discovered at the start of World War II and used as a bomb shelter for the

Kefalonia's Drogarati Cave

locals. It is a dry cave, well lit and with numbered formations with names suggested for their shapes. If one does not play the guessing game of what the formations look like, the trip is much quicker. However Santa Claus and the Kremlin are obvious. One emerges from the exit at the top of the hill, higher than the entrance, with a good view over Ioanina and the lake.

Halfway between Thessaloniki and Kassandra in **Halkidiki** are the caves of **Petralona**, where we were left alone to wander about. The cave was discovered during drilling to search for water in 1959. Iannis and Anna Petrohilos came to direct the investigations. All their finds are in a museum on site. There are some cave paintings here and the earliest evidence of the use of fire by humans (700,000 years ago). One of the earliest European pre-sapiens skulls was found here, c200,000 years old. The Great Hall is 104 x 12 metres and 8 metres high and there are the usual flowstone, stalagmite and stalactite formations but here coloured red due to mineral traces in the rocks.

16.5 km east of **Kalavrita** (SE of Patras and known for the German atrocity when the population was murdered) is the **Cave of Lakes** at **Kastria**. Close by is one of the increasing number of Greek ski resorts, Mt Helmos, so you can imagine we are quite high. The rack and pinion railway ascent from the Corinthian Gulf coast east of Aegion to Kalavrita is worth the trip itself. Pausanias refers to this cave in the 2nd century BC so it has always been well known. It is actually an underground river passage which gathers water from potholes around and emerges as a river some 8km away. The passage now operates as 13 large terraced lakes fed by snow melt and largely drying up in summer, revealing the lacework of stone basins and dams up to 4m deep. Whilst the cave was known, its extent was not established until 1964 when the ubiquitous Anna Petrohilos directed the mapping of the cave. The explored length is 1980 metres but only 350 metres can be visited and has been operated as a tourist attraction since 1981. The cave is approached through 3 airlock type doors in an effort to minimise changes to the cave environment. There is a major concentration of bats in this cave and for the first time in my life I heard bats, not just their wings but their echolocation chirping. The lighting has made the most of the formations and the route on man-made bridges over the lakes has utilised the water's reflections to enhance the display.

Another cave known from ancient times is of course **Zeus cave** (Diktaion Antron) on **Crete** where the infant Zeus was said to have been hidden. This is being archaeologically explored so access is restricted, but the setting gives an excellent view of the Omalos plateau in the centre of Crete.

25km from **Drama**, Macedonia, are the **Caves of Alistrati**. As with many caves they were known to locals as places of refuge. In 1959 a school geography trip penetrated deeper than the locals had, and in 1975 a local (on a return home from Athens) explored the caves and persuaded the council that they had an asset that needed further investigation by experts. There are 5 caves in the district covering 25,000 square metres and 3,000 metres in length. Scientific exploration continued for some years and the caves opened to the public in 1998. The fossilised fauna remains date back 2 million years, the main passage is 1200 metre long and the main chamber is 60 x 100 metres 20-30 metres high and there are helectites (solid club-like shapes), heccentrites (spreading out in many directions), as well as curtain-like stalagmites and stalactites, tubular stalactites and colourful red 'flames' up to 15 metres long.

Finally, back to the Ionian, there are more caves in **Kefalonia**. You might worry that a seismically active area is unlikely to retain its caves, but **Drogarati** (photo p95), revealed after an earthquake 300 years ago, is 100 million years old. It is south of Sami and has impressive formations of flowstone.

Midday Mist on Kefalonia's Melisani lake and tourist boats

The main chamber of 900 square metres has been used for concerts. Also on Kefalonia is the **Melissani cave**, a water filled void where the roof of the cave has worn through to the surface (a crown hole) and the boat ride round the lake is illuminated from above. At midday the sun is warm enough and directly overhead to create a mist on the surface of the underground lake which is quite impressive. It was on this tour that I first noticed the Greek guide technique (bearing in mind I have only restaurant Greek) of *"Gabble, gabble. Gabble, gabble, gabble, gabble. Gabble,gabble. Gabble, gabble, gabble, gabble, gabble"* in Greek for about 3 minutes then in English just *"5 metres"*. Clearly there was a lot more being said to those who understood the native Greek.

So, if you want somewhere cool (constant 16-20°C) when the heat is high, look for your nearest Greek cave and be awed by the natural formations and the Greek guide's entertainment.

Greece is four dimensional - the fourth dimension being time. Greek caves extend that dimension backwards like time capsules.

A number of short pieces were submitted from people who visited Ormos Marathokambou, Samos in 2003. Two, plus another photograph, are presented here and the poem 'What do they Talk about?' is in the Life in Greece section - together they paint an endearing impression of this part of Samos and its people.

Samos Revisited *by Mary Lambell*

Having holidayed in **Kokkari** (Κοκκάρι) in the north of Samos first in 1999, then visited on overnight stops at the beginning and end of a holiday on Patmos in 2002, our appetite was whetted for another Samos holiday. In September 2003 we decided to try a different area and chose **Ormos Marathokambou** (Όρμος Μαραθοκάμπου) on the south west coast, near to the highest mountain on Samos, **Kerketeas** (Ορος Κερκετέας), at 1434 metres. This is a traditional fishing village where tourism is low-key, and most inhabitants stay through the winter. There are five or six tavernas along the harbour side where you can sit and watch the fishing boats come in with their catches. The fish we ate was so fresh that one of them in the cold cabinet where we made our choice was still moving.

The fishing season officially began on 1st October, when catches of larger fish were permitted. There was supposed to be a festival in Ormos on the following Saturday, with singing and dancing, but it had to be postponed till the next week. The reason? A teachers' strike! The two local dancers were teachers. Because they were on strike on Monday and Tuesday they decided to take a long weekend away, so would not be available. This could only happen in Greece. I trust the festival went ahead the next week, but we were home by then.

In a remote village called **Kosmadei** (Κοσμαδαίοι) from where we had walked to a tiny monastery, we went into a kafeneion for lunch. We ordered omelettes, but were given two plain fried eggs each. They were delicious and had come from the hens we had just passed on our walk. On asking for the 'toualetta' we were shown a small building outside with a carpet for a door. The flushing mechanism was a large metal drum filled with water, and a container to scoop it up. On the slope just below was a small garden filled with very healthy courgette plants!

In another village, **Kastanea** (Καστανέα) we were greeted by a very smartly dressed man saying *"Welcome to our village"*. When we told him we were staying in Ormos he replied, *"I used to run the pizza place there. Now my brother-in-law runs it."* Of course we had to eat there that night and tell them why. On the strength of it we were both given a *"special drink"*.

We enjoyed a guided walk in **Marathokambos** (Μαραθόκαμπος), up the hill from its beachside counterpart, often called just Ormos, the bay. A local teacher, Kostas, gave us a fascinating tour of the village, telling us something of its history and its people. The tour was punctuated by his knocking on the doors of his friends who lived there, including the mayor. Because Kostas' enthusiasm kept us in the town longer than planned we ended up walking down through olive groves to **Votsalakia** (Βοτσαλάκια) on the coast in the dark well before we reached the end. It was quite difficult to see our way, but we had an excellent meal awaiting us in the local taverna.

A boat trip with one of the local fishermen had the added interest of an explanation of the various fish he had caught in the net he had let down the previous night. These formed part of the lunch cooked for us on a deserted beach - the famous 'Picnic trip' with which other readers may be familiar.

Did we notice any differences since our last visit? More roads had been surfaced, such as the direct road to Ormos from the airport. The terrible fires of 2000 had devastated some areas, which will take years to recover, but fortunately others were untouched. After the fires the Free Volunteers of Marathokambos came into being. A second-hand fire engine was bought, with the help of donations from Laskarina clients, which has subsequently been used to put out small fires in the area. Samos has a smart new air terminal opened in June 2003, with plenty of room to sit. The areas we revisited, like the Valley of the Nightingales and Evpalinos' Tunnel, did not seem any more busy - in fact we almost had the tunnel to ourselves.

Sometimes it can be a disappointment to return to a place you have enjoyed, but this was not the case with Samos. The best things were unchanged - the food, the wine, the 'philoxenia', the spectacular scenery.

Walk to Ormos & Island Tour *by Jenny Booth*

Our first trip to Samos was enjoyable, but at first we found it difficult to come to terms with the size of the island having more recently holidayed on smaller islands - Skiathos, Santorini, Alonnissos, Kalymnos and Paxos. However, once we had discovered how good the walking is (despite the awful fire damage, including some very recent) and the delights of the many inland villages (paid only €1 for a large Mythos beer at The Blue Chairs, Vourliotes) we were able to reconcile ourselves to the size.

We used the Sunflower Landscapes guide as our bible and managed to clock up many walking miles, using taxis and buses at either end. The buses ran to the winter timetable late in September, but were still reasonably frequent and they ran to time.

One day we decided to start a walk effectively from the middle of nowhere (just a name on the map, with a taverna) so asked a taxi driver for **Koutsi** (Κουτσι). The conversation went something like this:

"Could you take us to Koutsi please?"

"Koutsi?"

"Yes Koutsi."

"Koutsi?"

Colin..... *"Show him on the map. I told you we should have just shown him the map."*

Frantic search for map....

"Yes, I know Koutsi but why you want to go there?"

*"Because we want to walk to **Ormos Marathokambos**."*

"Why. Are you staying there?"

"No, we are staying here....."

Very puzzled look.

"..... we will catch the bus back."

"I could take you there in the taxi. ... Why do you want to walk?"

"It's what we do."

"OK"

... After about 10 minutes ...

"I still don't understand."

Colin...... *"Crazy English."*

"Ah!"

This seemed to resolve matters to the taxi driver's satisfaction.

The walk was excellent, but timing was crucial as the bus back was a very infrequent service and, if we missed it, we would have been looking at a very expensive taxi fare. We did catch the bus and it was full - but what a journey! It took about 2 hours in all, but we effectively got an island tour for about €4 each. We had to traverse the island from south to north then from west to east mainly along the coast road to arrive in Samos town where we caught our connection back to **Pythagorio** in the southeast.

At one point, the driver unexpectedly stopped the bus and pulled over to the opposite side of the road. The passengers were eager to discover why. Was there a problem? No, not a problem, just the driver, then the conductor stopping to do their shopping. There was a man selling fish from the back of a van. Having made their purchases the journey resumed .... Only in Greece!

So now we are back home. The tan is covered up and all we have to see us through until Skopelos next June is reading material and photographs!

Traffic Calming Measures *from Derek Robson*

This photograph illustrates the very effective traffic calming measures witnessed on Samos, Pythagorio to Pirgos road. I understand this method is being studied with a view to adopting it across the EU. As a keen gardener I look forward to the day.

Being 'our' island, we wrote about western Lesvos and Eresos in our Greek-o-File Introductory Issue, leaving 'the other side' for later. Here we print reader articles about northeast and central Lesvos where most tour operator holidays are based, leaving the capital Mytilene, east & southeast for possible future publications.

Profile of NE & Central Lesvos *by Sylvia Cook*

Visitors to Lesvos are often surprised at its size (the third largest Greek island) and its contrasting areas. The northeast corner is very green with much unspoilt countryside ideal for walkers, botanists and bird watchers. Red-tiled houses cluster in fairly large villages separated by large areas of olive groves, forest and farmland. **Mt. Lepetimnos** (Oρ. Λεπέτυμνος)  rises to 968m between **Madamados** (Μανταμάδος) and the ancient coastal town of **Mithymna** (Μήθυμνα), also known by its Turkish name **Molyvos** (Μόλυβος). Turkey dominated this island for many centuries, and is clearly visible from the coast on most days. From the northern beaches of **Petra** (Πέτρα) and **Anaxos** (Άναξος) the road winds up through olive groves and down to the plains and salt pans of the central town of **Kalloni** (Καλλονή) and its coastal resort on the **Gulf of Kalloni**. Inland villages, particularly the larger ones - Madamados (famous for pottery), **Stipsi** (olive oil), **Filia, Ag. Paraskevi** - see few tourists, but are worth a visit if you like to get off the beaten track. Be aware that inland village kafeneions and tavernas may be shut during the afternoon siesta.

Adapted from Efstathiadis Road Atlas

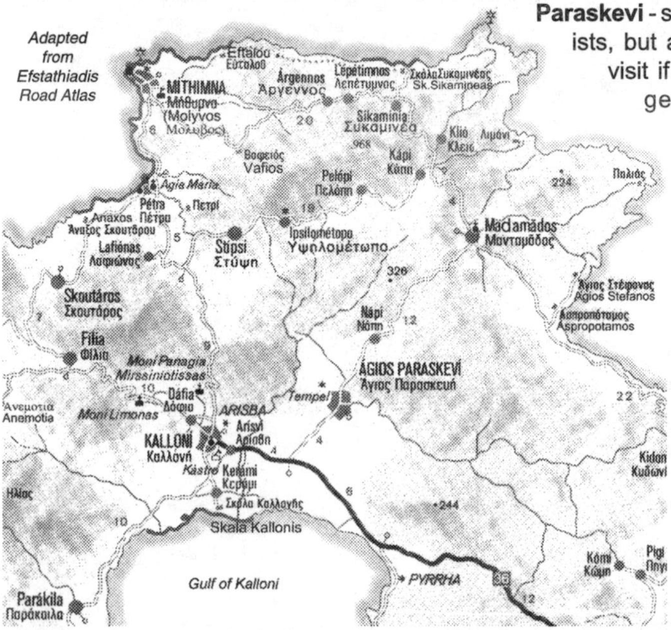

NE & Central Lesvos Background

☐ *__Mithymna__ and __Arisvi__ were two of the 5 ancient towns of Lesvos, named after king Makareus' children around 11th c.BC. The Mithymna area was occupied from the Bronze Age. Historically it was an important town, often competing with Mytilene for supremacy. Today's hilltop castle, on an ancient site, was built in Byzantine times, extended by the Genoese (in 1373AD) and during the long Turkish occupation.*

☐ *Being so close there was a particularly strong Turkish influence to architecture until 1923, when the Turks living in Lesvos were sent back to Asia Minor in exchange for Greeks living there.*

☐ *The fascinating __Taxiarchis Monastery__ outside __Madamados__ has a black icon (made from bloodied soil after a massacre of monks) visited by many pilgrims. On the annual feast weekend late April many people walk from as far as Mytilene or Kalloni to ask favours before feasting on the 'sacrificed' bull, enjoying the street market and meeting friends.*

☐ *The __Limonas Monastery__ above Kalloni was founded 1527, during the Turkish occupation, but has been enlarged considerably since.*

Postcards from Petra *by Angela Buchanan*

This is the diary of myself and teenage daughter Alice, when we ventured on a week's holiday to Lesvos, leaving 'brave volunteer' Stewart (husband and dad) behind with Max, our elderly dog, who we would not put in kennels as he now needs much care and medication. In the past Max has stayed with friends and relatives, but that was not possible this time.

We decided to go somewhere we had been before, **Petra** in Lesvos. After a tearful farewell at Manchester airport (well, we had never been separated for a whole week before!), we left Stewart behind and flew off to warmer climes, promising to keep in touch. (Edited highlights of a relaxing Greek holiday)

Dear Stewart/Daddy,   *Thurs. 13th July*

Plane 2 hours late taking off! Drive to Petra seemed long after early morning start. We nodded off some of the time. Saw local fire brigade in their usual spot sitting under shade on hill overlooking the island forestry. Passed the turning for Roman aqueduct where we got lost last visit and scraped the hire car. Hotel  is excellent, clean and people very obliging. Family run - Australian mother married to Greek with 2 good looking strapping sons to help. They also have a pet dog called Lucy running around.

Had swim in pool after late lunch and large beer, then sleep. Good vegetarian dinner here - aubergine with cheese topping, mixed veg and chips then Greek yoghourt and honey. Walked into village to phone you. Had a drink at Bros Taverna. It's very hot. Sweating like a pig but will try to sleep. Love and miss you loads. xxxx A&A

Dear Stewart/Daddy   *Fri. 14th July*

Breakfast not as good as last year but good hot tea, juice, bread, jam, cheese & cake. 'Welcome' meeting 10am wasn't too long or boring. Decided not to go on any trips. Might have gone to Mytilene, but it was shops OR museums and we wanted both! Lazy day by pool.

Good lunch - generous portions. Chatted with woman here with her 80-year old mother, third time at this hotel. Dinner was tuna salad, potatoes and beans swimming in that lovely tomato & oil sauce. Walked into Petra. Alice bought silver dolphin ring. Got in 10pm. Going to sleep now. xxx A&A

Dear Stewart/Daddy   *Sat. 15th July*

Injuries to date: One stubbed toe, purple & a bit swollen, only hurts a bit (caught the bed leg going to bathroom in middle of night!); Ten huge red mosquito bites on legs - left repellent at home, but bought some, too late I fear. Today's breakfast - an egg. Taxi into **Molyvos** to see shops & harbour today. Good lunch halfway up hill from harbour - good price. Saw silver bracelet, bit expensive but might go back for it. Alice bought another ring, I bought olive soap, Greek Delights & new playing cards. Spent afternoon at pool back at hotel. Walked into Petra after dinner to phone you & bought Grandma her cigs. All our love A&A xxx

Dear Stewart/Daddy   *Sun. 16th July*

Lazy day by pool. Late morning short walk to marina and looked for fish. I stayed in shade all day, Alice sunbathed and had a nap before dinner. Camera batteries given up - must buy more tonight. Into Petra after good Greek dinner. Seen another bracelet, a lot cheaper. Need to decide which one to get. Saw owl on way

back. 10.45 on balcony. I can hear village concert just down the road, noisy but at least it's Greek rather than disco music. It's going to be a long night! Love you. A&A xxx

Dear Stewart/Daddy   *Mon. 17th July*

Had a walk after breakfast to find a donkey and her new baby we'd heard about. They were other end of bay by Clara Hotel where we stayed before. Called in for refreshing drink - but nothing available 10.20am. Pool bar not open and some people still eating breakfast. Had game of pool and rest in shade. Fed mother donkey some water melon on way back. Stopped again at first taverna for frappe & Fanta. On to Panayia Glykofiloussa (church on rock). Greek coach party just arrived. Busy! Lunch at Bros. Lazed by pool all afternoon. Just finished reading second book - I'd bought another in Molyvos. Another good dinner, walk to shops and phone. Bought beach towel for Jack. Alice bought a necklace. Love you A&A xxx

Dear Stewart/Daddy   *Tues. 18th July*

Very hot last night, tossed & turned a bit. Ready to come home for a cuddle! Taxi into Molyvos today. Climbed all those steps to the castle. Wind blew my hat off. Found it on way back down on head of a small Greek boy! With my limited Greek I managed to get it back. Bought the expensive bracelet, but was given special price! Drink stop overlooking Molyvos bay then back to hotel for afternoon by pool. Alice played with 2 girls there all afternoon so felt a bit lonely - aah! BBQ night at hotel - salad, beans, tzatziki fine; chicken and chops for meat eaters; dog sick for us! I think it was the artichoke omelette that had gone badly wrong! Decided to recover with tea and cakes in Petra. Bumped into someone from our hotel so stopped for chat. Finally in bed 11.15pm. Alice says she can't wait to see you & misses you lots. Me too! Looking forward to coming home. A&A xxxx

Dear Stewart/Daddy   *Wed. 19th July*

Last night in Petra. Both looking forward to seeing you again. Short walk after breakfast. Back to pool for morning. Wanted to snorkel near marina but too choppy. Bought picnic lunch in Petra - baguette and spinach pie. Ate it on benches near the square. Walked back & stayed by pool, Alice with friends again. Dinner, then into Petra for last look at shops. On way back saw a firefly. Love you very much - see you tomorrow. A&A xxx

All Roads Lead to Eftalou *by Glenn R. Steiner*

The donkey man tipped his black fisherman's hat and swatted his quadruped with a reed whip. His donkey took off with a jolt, clip-clopping down the path to **Skala Sykaminias** (Σκ.Συκαμινιάς). An errant breeze swirled the dust about the donkey's hooves. Loose rocks cascaded down the yellow slopes of Cape Karkouras, to the straights of Lesvos far below.

The early glow of the new sun crested the Turkish mainland some 12 kilometres distant. I squinted, wiping trailing sweat trickling from my brow. My vision fuzzed slightly. Man and donkey rounded the bend, merging in the morning light into one being.

"Wasn't his name Chiron," queried Rose. I had to smile. Chiron was the mythical centaur and great teacher of the warrior Achilles.

With a final wave of his reed whip, held high in salute, a silhouetted Chiron rambled out of sight. The staccato of footfalls and flying stones echoed; the odd syncopation slowly supplanted by the surf's growing surge and quickening breeze.

The pre-morning journey had started from Skala Sykaminias, a small harbour northwest of Molyvos and legendary home of The Mermaid Madonna of Greek literary fame - one of my favourite stories. It tells of a painter washed up on this Lesvos' shore. Within the local chapel, which stands defiantly on the breakwater of the harbour, he painted a mysterious mermaid icon. The Mermaid Madonna protected and watched over the locals and immigrants  from Turkey, subtly changing and influencing their lives.

Having started early in the morning, Rose and I had hopped on our moped and sped off on the dirt trail. Looking back, I stole a glance, watching the harbour lights of Skala Sykaminias reflect off the wine dark sea. Night time riding had its downfalls. The Stygian darkness and lack of a full moon had soon disoriented us. We'd have even accepted help from a Centaur.

Eftalou (Εφταλού) came to us, as if in a dream, shrouded in mists, super-naturally bright. The stone building itself stood out below the sea cliffs, small in stature. Yet, this ancient Lesvian site of spiritual healing seemed more expansive. We shed our dusty mopeds and entered.

A small blue wooden door opened. A spry small German woman of indeterminate age smiled, bidding us welcome. *"My name is Hilda."*

Rose marvelled at Hilda's glowing health and radiant skin.

"I came here many years ago, to find my centre." Vapours smelling gently of sulphur drifted from an interior door.

"The waters here are volcanic and heated to 43° centigrade. Lesvos has always been rich in minerals. And so, the earth has saturated the waters with iron, magnesium, calcium, lithium, sodium, potassium, aluminium sulphate, magnesium and manganese. First, you must shower outside and then, return to the cave."

Rose and I left our belongings in a locker and stepped outside into the now blinding light of the new born sun. The shower flowed from a local spring out of the cliff's side. Sweet, cool spring waters swept the morning dust from our bodies and hair. We stumbled back up the beach of pebbly round rocks.

An opaque mist shrouded the cave's entrance. Someone of Hilda's elflike size could easily enter. Rose looked at me and smiled. I was almost twice Hilda's size. Genuflecting low by half, Rose parted the mists and crept into the cave of Eftalou. All I saw were her footprints down the short moist steps. I followed close on her heels and smacked my head on the ceiling.

My eyes adjusted. The room appeared to expand. Candles filled pockmarks in the foot-thick, stone walls. It seemed less a cave, more a shrine, a place of private worship. The air lay thick with superheated moisture. We slipped very, very slowly into the pool, starting first with just the tips of our toes. The heat was incandescent, volcanic. Rose withdrew suddenly. I continued, my toes, my heels, my ankles, my knees consumed with fire. The burning grew too intense. I withdrew too and we rested on the comparatively cool stone ledge. Two spring lobsters too young to cook, we took deep breaths and slipped back into the pools. Strangely, the waters grew not hotter, but less. I slid slowly into opalescent waters, smelling slightly of brimstone. For a moment I could not breathe. I opened my eyes. The mists had transformed the cave into a barrel-vaulted basilica. Holes cut into the stone roof for ventilation threw bolts of fire, long broadswords of blinding light, which danced through the ethers of air and water.

From somewhere, the voice of Enya grew and retreated, drifting on butterfly wings. I became aware of the slow beating of my heart, and breathed deep the mists of Eftalou. In mid-muse, I saw Rose bolt from the black pool. I

followed, running out into the morning light, down the stony beach. We threw ourselves into the ocean.

We were reborn! The steep, short, wind driven swells pushed and pulled at our naked bodies. The superheated waters mixed with the cool Aegean of May. We swam and dove as porpoises. Immersed in the saltine sea, fingers of warmth caressed us.

What would the ancients have made of this? I pondered. Would this be their mystic Eleusis, the rite of winter turning into spring, symbolising the rescue of Persephone from Hades?

We crawled up the stone filled slope on all fours, up to the shower. The return to the black pool was sublime. Amazingly, we slid in up to our necks with little discomfort. Closing my eyes, I ducked my head beneath. The sharpness of the heat demanded a quick withdrawal. Bursting free, I could see sunlight, burning pinpoints, miniature suns that danced on the surface.

Another dip in the now warm sea outside refreshed us. Yet, parting time had come. Showering and dressing, we bid diminutive Hilda a fond *"Yeia sou"* and started back along the roadside trail.

Molyvos' (Mithymna) hilltop castle looms

Ancient **Mithymna** crowned with its wonderful Genoese castle lay before us some miles distant.

The words of an old philosophy professor suddenly ran through my mind. I smiled, and looked into Rose's pale blue-green eyes. *"Time is a river. It flows at its own speed. You cannot pull at it. You cannot push it, although sometimes it seems faster. If you try to impede its progress, it flows through your fingers and resumes its own course."* I gave her a hug.

The waters of Eftalou lay behind us. The morning sun was beating down. Doves *"coo-coo"*-ed from Tamarisk trees. The Turkish winds brought scents of lemon and sage across the straights of Mytilene.

For the life of me, I still can't remember my moped touching the ground until we hit the cobbled streets of **Molyvos**.

Paradise Found in Skala Kallonis by Kath Riddell

I have been a 'Greece-a-holic' now for more years than I care to remember, ever since my parents took me and my sister on a tour of Classical Greece in 1975. In fact, I take full responsibility for introducing my friends Christine and Steve, who had never been to Greece, to Kos in 1992. Since then they have never looked back and are hooked as well. We try to visit Greece twice a year, sometimes returning to places and islands we have enjoyed and frequently trying new destinations. Together, we have visited at least 15 islands over the past few years, In September 2001 we tried one of our 'new' islands - Lesvos.

We booked ourselves a week in the fairly touristy, though small, resort of **Anaxos** (Άναξος) on the north coast. Being late season and quieter than the summer months, a most enjoyable time was had by all. We visited **Molyvos** and **Skala Sykaminias** and went on a 'villages' tour which involved walking through several small villages, including **Stipsi** (Στύψη) and **Pelopi** (Πελόπη), stopping to visit bakeries and kafeneia en route. The honey and cinnamon doughnuts we sampled were the best I have ever tasted. All too soon our week's holiday came to a close and we reluctantly boarded the coach for the airport. Our route took us back through the centre of the island and the small resort of **Skala Kallonis** (Σκ.Καλλονής), which lies at the head of the Gulf of Kalloni, just three kilometres from the town of the same name. We stopped to collect people in the square with its fountain, tavernas and cafes right by the harbour side. From that moment we were smitten! We were later to discover that

the square came alive at night with Greek families coming down from the town to dine in the restaurants there.

There are few companies offering this destination, but eventually we found and booked our two week holiday in Skala Kalloni for July 2003. Our accommodation was changed 2 months before we were due to go, but we needn't have worried. The Marianna, just behind the square, was superb, set amidst fields where the owners kept their sheep, goats and chickens, with lovely views to three sides over the surrounding countryside. We enjoyed the sunrise over the bay from the rear of our rooms and the sunset from our large balconies at the front.

We met and made friends with several local people, Stella and Stavros who owned our apartments, Captain Panos who ran the cruises, Nicos the baker, who slipped Greek sweets into the bag with our bread each morning, Iannis who owned the Family bar where we spent most eve-  nings and was the nearest thing to a kafeneion we could find. It certainly had the usual absence of women, apart from a few visitors like ourselves. It was here we met Dimitri who was 84. We used to call him 'Mr Happy Face' because that described him perfectly. He didn't speak any English and as I have only just started to learn Greek, we got by in the usual manner of much arm waving and pointing to our Greek phrase book. There was Penny and her husband George who ran the Paradise Bar on the beach serving the coldest and the best big beers, and we even had a local pelican. We hired a car for five days in the middle of our holiday and spent the time travelling round to **Sigri** (Σίγρι), **Andissa** (Άντισσα), **Vatera** (Βατερά), **Molyvos** and **Anaxos** once again, just to see if it had changed.

We sampled captain Panos' cruises, the first a BBQ, where Panos and his crew mate carried sun loungers and umbrellas from the boat, through the sea to the beach for us. The second was a 'sunset cruise', when we actually missed the sunset because some people arrived late. Then, because of rough seas, the return journey that should have taken about 50 minutes took 2½ hours and we finally docked at 2.30 am. We were kept warm by several large glasses of ouzo and birthday cake, bought by Panos, for one gentleman whose birthday just happened to fall on that day. As we pulled into the harbour, one of our fellow travellers commented that he was sure he'd booked for a sunset not a sunrise cruise! The evening before we left, I gave my 'England' sun hat to Dimitri, which he proudly insisted on wearing straight away. Our time there passed far too quickly and we vowed to return as soon as we could.

Back home, I spent hours trying in vain to find our Marianna Apartments on the Internet, so that we could return in September. I was becoming really despondent, when I came across a Lesvos travel company based in Molyvos and discovered to my joy that they could book our apartments for us. Flights arranged, we set off with great excitement and anticipation on the 25th of September. Imagine my delight, when on walking down the street leading

to the square, on the afternoon of our arrival, there was Dimitri sitting with his England hat on, by now very faded from the sun and dusty with use. We were welcomed like long lost brothers and sisters by all our newly found friends and felt so 'at home'.

This time we ventured up to the town of **Kalloni** and sat watching the world go by at a kafeneion in the main street, while drinking the usual Mythos (or three). When the time came for us to return to the UK, we were given bottles of ouzo by Dimitri, ouzo glasses from Iannis and bread from Nicos the baker.

I felt very sad to be leaving our little corner of paradise once again and not a day goes by when I don't think with a smile of the wonderful holidays we spent and the friends we made in Skala Kallonis.

How to get to Lesvos

By Air - Scheduled flights via Athens, Chios, Limnos, Rhodes, Thessaloniki & UK Charters direct May to October.

By Ferry - links with Alexandropoli, Chios, Kavala, Kos, Limnos, Mykonos, Piraeus, Rhodes, Samos, Syros, Thessaloniki, Tinos.

Tour Operators - Airtours, Direct Greece, Filoxenia, First Choice, Greek Tourism-Travel, Hidden Greece, Island Wandering, Kosmar, Libra, Limosa (birdwatching), Manos, Naturetrek, Simply Travel, Sunvil.

A Trip to the Beach *by Fiona Collingwood*

Yiorgos, our young son Timothy and I moved to **Volos** (Βολος) in September, when the weather is still warm and the sea a perfect temperature for swimming.

September is my favourite month in Greece, when it is starting to cool down (much to my relief, as August is usually a scorcher with temperatures often reaching 40°C), most foreign and Greek tourists are going home and the pace of life seems to slow down. The tourist shops, summer bars and clubs start to close for winter and the children reluctantly go back to school leaving the beaches behind. If you visit one of the blue flag beaches in the east of the **Pelion** peninsular, the chances are you might just have it all to yourself.

After weeks of unpacking and rearranging we'd had enough of being indoors. We needed to escape. Yiorgos suggested we visit **Aghios Ioannis** (Αγ. Ιωάνης) in north eastern Pelion, about 55 kms from Volos.

We decided to take the route over the mountains as opposed to the coast road and cutting across via **Milies** (Μηλιές). We had plenty of time free, so we could take a leisurely trip, stopping wherever it pleased us. The plan was to drive up to Portaria, then to Chania, the ski resort near the peak, then it would be down hill all the way to Makryrachi, Anilio and finally to Aghios Ioannis.

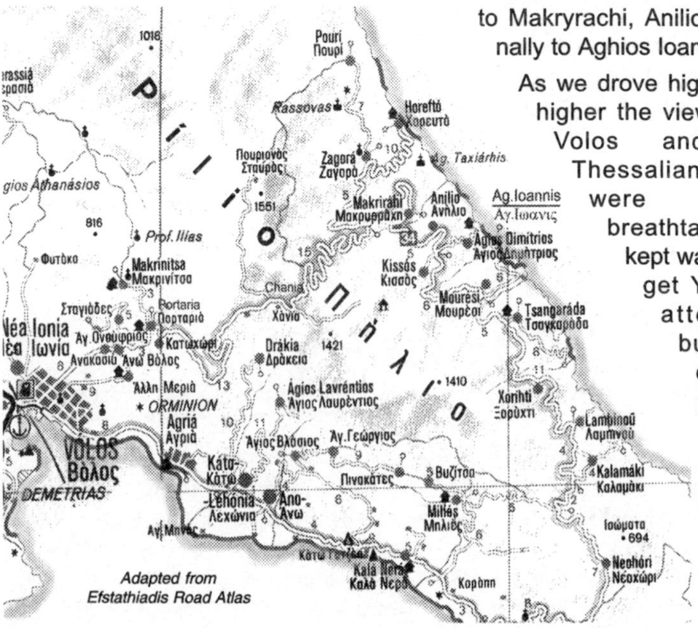

As we drove higher and higher the views over Volos and the Thessalian plain were simply breathtaking. I kept wanting to get Yiorgos' attention, but his eyes were sensibly firmly fixed on the road which twisted

Adapted from
Efstathiadis Road Atlas

Portaria

and turned with sheer drops alongside at several points.

We pressed on through the village of **Portaria** (Πορταριά) and continued up to **Chania** (Χάνια). I began to realise that the Pelion, my new Greek home, is undoubtedly one of the most beautiful and unspoilt regions in the country. It is very different from the islands of the Aegean which tend to be seen as archetypal of Greece. You won't see small white sugar cube houses or churches with azure domed roofs, windmills on rocky promontories or the barren landscapes of some islands. Instead the houses cling to the fertile mountainside, often one storey at the back and three at the front, the upper storey projecting outwards, usually half timbered. The Pelion house has a grey slate roof, ornate intricately carved wooden doors, balconies and shutters. Inside is the same attention to detail with wooden floors and ceilings, the latter often carved then painted.

As we passed through the villages we noticed the houses nestling amongst lush flora virtually camouflaged from sight. Each village is fed by crystal clear streams which network their way from village to village. We stopped at several roofed wells to fill up our water bottles, as the water was pure and icy fresh.

Our senses were overloaded. We saw orchards, olive groves and vineyards for miles around. We could hear running water, bird song, church bells and the faint tinkling of goats' bells. A variety of aromas assaulted our noses from all directions - meat cooking on the spit, fresh cheese bread and walnut cakes from the bakeries and the smell of thyme, oregano, sage and chamomile from the mountainsides.

As we drove under the canopy of trees after Chania, the air temperature dropped and after more hairpin bends and winding roads we arrived at **Makryrachi** (Μακρυρράχη) and next **Anilio** (Ανήλιο). These are typical of villages in the Pelion - old cobbled streets, 18th century mansion houses and usually a village square with a huge plane tree as a focal point providing shade for the customers of the kafeneia and tavernas scattered around

the periphery. Tradition and culture are paramount and many of the villages have not changed much for hundreds of years. Sipping an ouzo under one of the old plane trees (some said to be over 1000 years old) it is hard to believe we are in the 21st century.

After stretching our legs in Anilio - place without sun - named I suppose because of all the shady trees, we continued our journey and the descent to our destination.

Aghios Ioannis is one of the more commercial places in Pelion in that it does have some foreign tourists, however it is a million miles away from the commercialism of Rhodes, Corfu and other popular islands. You could say it is quiet. It has 3 beaches, one by the village itself, another called **Plaka** (Πλάκα), just 300 metres away and **Papa Nero** (Παπά Νερό) 1km away. All the beaches are excellent. The village has a promenade, the odd tourist shop, taverna and ouzerie, a few bars, but really not much else. The beaches are the main attraction.

Ag. Ioanis Main Beach

We headed for Plaka beach, which was a mini-paradise - a sandy beach with pebbles at the shoreline, edged with jungle-like vegetation. It felt more as if we were in the Far East than Greece. This beach was quiet as we had expected - just us and another family, probably locals. We made the most of the crystal clear sea, taking a dip immediately. The only problem was that it did get deep quickly, so after a while we headed back to the town beach where it was safer for our son to paddle.

After we'd had some time enjoying ourselves on this beach, we found a local taverna. We got carried away by the fantastic selection of *tapsi* (metal trays of food) to choose from - stuffed peppers, yiouvetsi, fish and potatoes, fassolakia (green beans), gigantes (giant white beans) to name but a few. Our greed overcame us. Finally, thoroughly stuffed we decided to postpone our drive back and booked into the rooms above the taverna so that we could enjoy a delicious meal again tomorrow and another great day at the beach.

Profile of Kalymnos *by Tim Horler*

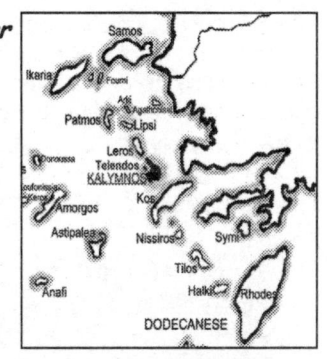

One of the Dodecanese Islands, **Kalymnos** (Κάλυμνος) is 110 sq km of mainly bare limestone, situated between Kos and Leros, a few miles off the Turkish coast.

A large rock in the Aegean sea, its close neighbour Telendos was part of the island until an earthquake about 1500 years ago separated them. In doing so it created a sheltered area which is enjoyed by many regular visitors. **Myrties** (Μυρτιές) and **Masouri** (Μασούρι) are twin resorts geared to provide the summer visitors with all the facilities they may want - comfortable rooms, pleasant bars and tavernas serving local and international cuisine, sunshine, beaches, sea and the opportunity to watch the islanders go about their business.

The island capital, **Pothia** (Πόθια) is set in a valley and wraps itself around the busy harbour. Cafe bars and waterfront restaurants are plentiful and many a peaceful hour can be spent watching the comings and goings of ships and boats. The harbour, once

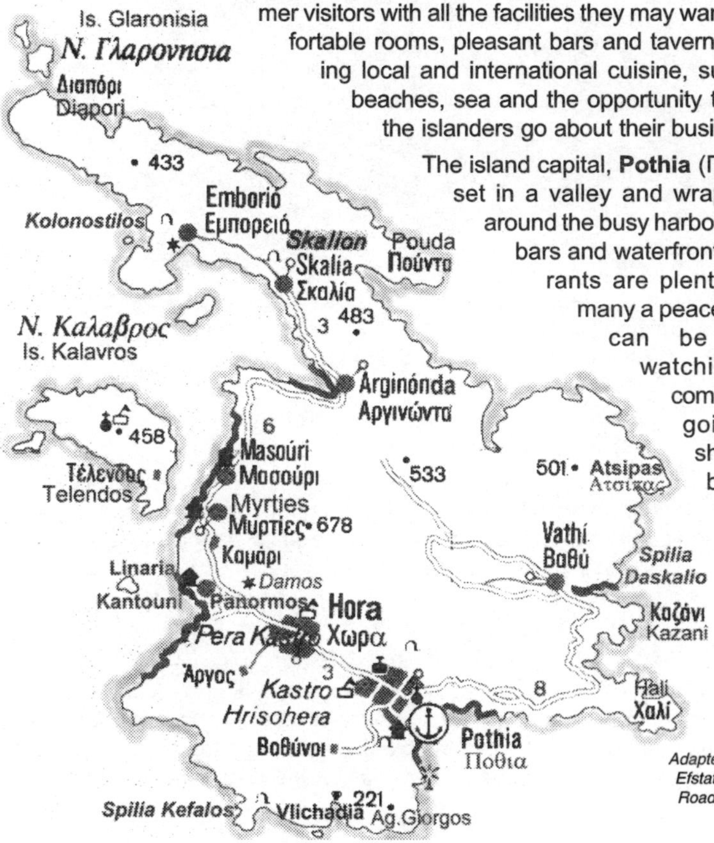

Is. Glaronisia
Ν. Γλαρονσια
Διαπόρι
Diapori

• 433

Emborió
Εμπορειό
Kolonostilos
Skalion Pouda
Skalía Πούντα
Σκαλία

Ν. Καλαβρος
Is. Kalavros
3 483

Arginónda
Αργινώντα

458
6
Masoúri
Μασούρι
533
501 • Atsipas
Ατσιπας

Τέλενδος
Telendos
Myrties
Μυρτιές • 678
Καμάρι
Vathí
Βαθύ
Spilia
Daskalio

Linaria
★ *Damos*
Kantouni Panormos **Hora**
Pera Kastro Χωρα
Καζάνι
Kazani

Άργος
3
Kastro
Hrisohera
8
Hali
Χαλί

Βαθύνοι
Pothia
Πόθια

Spilia Kefalos Vlichadia 221
Ag. Giorgos

Adapted from Efstathiadis Road Atlas

the main home of the sponge fishing fleet, is the first thing most visitors see, as the airport on the island is yet to be completed. The houses are mostly painted white, many with the typical blue painted woodwork reflecting the colours of the Greek flag. People here are fiercely proud of their heritage and national pride is strong. They are glad to welcome visitors and those who return year after year are treated as family. Just around the coast south from the main port of Pothia, **Vlichadia** bay is sheltered on three sides and is generally quieter than other bays. It has just two tavernas and a bar.

Vlichadia
Bay

Vathi (Βαθύ) is in a fertile valley which enjoys a good fresh water supply. It was once explained to me that Kalymnos was named because of this water supply and its importance to mariners as an island to visit to replenish their supplies. Today Vathi is the garden of the island, growing fresh vegetables and fruit. There are many orchards of mandarin oranges and the smell of them in late summer is zesty and fresh.

Kantouni (Καντούνη) and **Linaria** (Λινάρια) are bays with sandy beaches and blue seas on the west coast. This area is popular with families as the beach slopes gently and the waves are good to play in. **Panormos** (Πάνορμος) with its busy square and shops is adjacent to **Hora** (Χώρα), the old town, the inland area where many locals live and work. **Skalia** (Σκαλία), **Emborio** (Εμπορειό) and **Arginonda** (Αργινώντα) are quiet villages on the north west coast with sandy beaches and welcoming facilities.

Telendos Isle (N. Τέλενδος), just off the west coast, is a tranquil place - no cars nor roads ensure it stays a truly peaceful location. During the winter months only half a dozen or so people live there and during the summer there does not seem to be many more. It's a real discovery for those who appreciate quiet.

Kalymnos Background *by Sylvia Cook*

☐ *Kalymnos has been inhabited since Neolithic times, yet not played any major part in history. Generally the island has followed the pattern of rule in neighbouring Dodecanese islands.*

☐ *Before 4th century BC the island was called Kalydnos, meaning 'well watered' from καλος (kalos - good) and υδωρ (ydor - water).*

☐ *Its main claim to fame is as an important centre for the sponge diving industry, although today the fleets are much depleted owing to scarcity of sponges in nearby waters. Kalymnians developed amazing underwater prowess to spear many sponges on one breath of air, before early diving suits allowed them to dive deeper (late 19th century), but many suffered death or brain damage from rising too quickly from the underwater pressure, before the problem was fully understood.*

☐ *The **Nautical & Folklore Museum** in Pothia charts life in recent history including the sponge fishing industry and the second World War.*

☐ *The neighbouring islet of **Imia,** used by some Kalymnos farmers to graze goats, was the cause of a major incident in 1996 when its ownership was disputed by Turkey.*

Kalymnos, The First Time *by Tim Horler*

"Where are you going on holiday this summer?" asked Pad. We hadn't thought much about it - well, it was still December, raining and with Christmas on its way other things occupied us. *"Why?"* I asked. *"We're going back to that Greek island and want you to come too."* *"Hmmmm."*

Pad practised his patter on us and others a few times. Result - the following September found twelve of us setting off from Somerset to Gatwick, to spend a fortnight on a large rock in Greece.

The old minibus he had managed to book for us arrived at 1 am and eventually got us to Gatwick, where we were led by sign boards and announcements, after queuing and waiting. We boarded the metal tube which accelerated us to 500 mph heading south east. Paddy had neglected to tell us he is petrified of flying. I have never seen such white knuckles or a seat belt pulled so tightly.

In the days before in-flight entertainment, there was little to do to pass the 2 hours after the cabin staff had finished bar runs, meals and, do you remember duty free? You could save a few quid on 200 ciggies, or wait until you landed to save even more.

"Captain here. We are beginning our descent." The air speed indicator climbed to 625 mph. *"I thought he said max speed was 500"* said Pad. He

pulled his seat belt even tighter. I didn't know anyone could hold their breath for 20 minutes.

Out of the porthole-size, misted up window I strained my eyes for my first view of Greek soil. Hmmm. The summer sun had scorched the earth and the scrub looked tired and longing for rain. Stepping out of the dim, cool cabin onto the stairs I was hit in the face by the heat and light. It took me by surprise.

The seasoned visitors made a dash in the hope of grabbing one of the 3 trolleys that were the total sum of customer baggage facilities. A queue was forming outside the toilet and there was a crush to reclaim luggage and get out of the oven that was the Kos airport arrivals hall.

We found the rep, then the coach that was to transport us to a waiting trans-fer boat, which we boarded after promising not to miss the welcome meet-ing. The coach roared off along the jetty, leaving part of its exhaust pipe behind, to meet the next flight bound for the same island. Being first on the boat we opted to sit on the small upper sun deck to enjoy the sea air. We got comfortable and waited, and waited, and waited - for around 2 hours for a delayed flight. When the coach finally returned a large cheer arose from the upper sun deck. The last passenger boarded and the coach departed leaving a few more pieces of exhaust behind. Once moving we felt the benefit of the upper deck, the steady warm sea breeze took the harshness of the heat away and the gentle rolling soon had us dozing.

Fifty minutes later we arrived at our island destination. The crew quickly unloaded our bags and were off to pick up a party of tourists they had dropped off for a beach picnic earlier, now 2 hours late.

Myrties & Massouri from Telendos Isle

A bus (?) arrived to collect us. To say someone had got their money's worth out of that vehicle is an understatement. The springs creaked and groaned with every piece of luggage and person loaded. *"They've done it up a bit since last time"* said Pad.

We set off through the main town. Small white houses on the hillside slopes gave way to shops and tavernas on the main roads. The narrow streets with washing hanging over balconies; carrier bags of bread on door handles; bags of rubbish on the pavements; few cars, but dozens of small motorcycles; the whole family riding on a Honda 50, mother side saddle and two children hanging on. *"What kind of place is this?"* we wondered.

We leave the town behind and head towards a small beach resort and our hotel in Massouri. The driver (in a fit of enthusiasm) reverses towards the hotel steps and into a girl on a motorcycle, knocking her off. Much shouting and gesticulating followed as the girl brushed herself off, got back on her bike and left. No exchange of details so I guess the incident went no further.

In the Hotel we were given keys to a room with twin beds. *"Right, where's the manager? We booked a double."* *"Swap with us"* offered Pad, so we did. It was now 5 pm and we'd been travelling for too long. A shower. Yes, good idea. I let the water run and run, but it remained cold. *"Right, where's the manager?"* *"I owner. You have problem?"*

"There is no hot water." *"OK, I show."*

Nick, as he introduced himself, came to the room and held his hand under the stream of water, twiddled the tap and said *"There, no problem."* It was still cold and I told him so. He maintained that it was warm, although his hand was turning blue. To avoid a Manuel/Basil Fawlty type conversation, I thanked him and took a cold shower.

We unpacked. We were new to the Greek Islands and had packed enough for a year. Our sun lotion stock was enough to supply a small shop. I took our tickets, passports and money to reception to put them in the safe.

Nick smiled at me. *"Another problem?"*

"Can you put these in the safe?" I held up my travel organiser pouch.

"Safe?" *"Yes, I want to put these in the safe."*

"What safe?" *"Somewhere to keep this where it won't get stolen."*

He took the pouch from me, threw it onto the shelf behind the reception desk, looked me in the eye and said *"SAFE!"*

It took me a few days to absorb the atmosphere, the people and the way of life - so different from home. Two weeks went far too quickly and we were not ready to return to reality when the holiday came to an end.

Since that first time we have returned every year, and now arrive with 4 children in tow. A feeling of calmness and peace now takes over whilst waiting to take off from the UK. We know that for the next week or two our hardest decisions will be where to eat and what to drink, so I arrive with my 'holiday head' on.

Myrties

Commercialism in its rudest form seems to have passed the island by, but tourist income has been used to improve many areas without destroying its charm. Old style values and hospitality live on. When Kalymnians say *"no problem"*, it is sincere and not a vague impersonal catch phrase like *"have a nice day"*. Children are welcomed in tavernas and bars and the absence of huge night clubs and loud disco bars deters the party animals and ravers from coming to the island.

Two years ago we started our own company to promote Kalymnos island and act as UK agent to small hotels and apartments, so our trips now are a mix of business and pleasure - but I still get a thrill when we arrive at the port and a sense of loss when we leave.

'Kalymnos, Island of Dreams' - it must be true, I read it on a t-shirt.

(See page 177 for details of Tim Horler's 'Fransway')

How to get to Kalymnos

By Air - Scheduled via Athens to Kos, Charter direct to Kos, then ferry.

By Ferry - links with Agathonissi, Amorgos, Astypalea, Fourni, Halki, Ikaria, Kos, Leros, Lipsi, Megisti, Naxos, Nissyros, Paros, Patmos, Piraeus, Rhodes, Samos, Symi, Syros, Tilos.

Tour Operators - Argo, First Choice, Fransway, Freedom of Greece, Greek Tourism-Travel, Hidden Greece, Island Wandering, Kosmar, Laskarina, Olympic Holidays, Ramblers.

Symphony on Hydra *by Glenn R. Steiner*

The morning sun wrapped its arms about me, reaching through my country window, gently shaking me awake. I pulled up the rough hewn, woollen blanket closer to my neck, listening. Not a single moped nor a single automobile could be heard, only the songs of animals, the laughter of children, I opened one eye and peered out. My friend, a big whiskered donkey that I nicknamed 'Pavarotti', nuzzled the window pane, fogging its surface with his breath. I smiled.

The morning symphony was just starting to warm up. A single church bell pealed, a single soprano sweetly spilling from its bell. A minute later from across the valley, another church's set of twin alto bells sang out. Then another church joined and yet another. Music cascaded across the hills of Italianate houses that ring the valley. I held my breath. My menagerie was not to be out done. The rooster started with his peremptory *"cock-a-doodle-DAAA"*. The hens clucked in concert. The neighbour's yappy dog barked and barked, baring its one good tooth joyously. The gray and white doves *"coo"*-ed loudly and sparrows *"cheap-cheap"*-ed. The herd of brown and white goats suddenly cried out in chorus. Pavarotti had nudged open the window. Then, as if rising to the barnyard challenge, Pavarotti threw back his enormous head, and let fly with a larger-than-life *"AWWW-HEEE-HAAAAW-HEEE-HAWWWWWWW "*.

Pavarotti's bray exploded into the room like a cannon shot. I levitated off the bed. All illusions of falling back to sleep had gone the way of the morning light. I threw on enough clothes to ward off the spring chill air, and set out to explore the day. In my wisdom after Poros, I had decided to find a *domatio* as far as possible from the town centre on **Hydra** (Ύδρα). Imagine that Hydra is shaped like a coffee cup, with the cutaway open at one end facing the sea. I lived about half way up the side of the bowl. The morning started with a hike down one hundred and forty two steep, marble steps. Whether there were plans and permits when the steps were originally cut remains lost in the mists of time. One didn't gently 'step' down in the Eng-

lish sense. One kind of jumped, using the adjacent buildings for additional purchase. The Hydriots, both young and old, sprang up and down their ancient staircases with the agility of mountain goats.

At the end of the steps, I turned right at the stately Hotel Aris, the last bastion for aristocracy. A cobblestone path of reddish and bluish rocks marked the way to town. The school's play yard and Hydra's miniature coliseum filled this part of the valley. From behind the perimeter wall, I heard the laughter and shouting of children at play. A breeze swept down from the mountain's crest, lifting a cluster of bougainvillea high into the air and then swirling the flowers forward. I meandered to the port, from one moment to the next surrounded by a halo of wind blown blossoms. I sat by my favourite *fournos* or bakery shop and ate the most sinfully, buttery croissant with fresh orange juice.

Ships of all descriptions filled Hydra's smallish, but energetic harbour. Colourful fishing caiques, a rusty World War II troop-landing ship, massive Sea Jet ferries, sleek Flying Dolphins and local transport ships worked the harbour's inner ring. The larger charter sailing boats and multi-million dollar mega yachts looked on from the outer periphery. Twenty three tavernas, untold trinket shops, rooms, hotels, gyros stands, jewellery stores, clothing emporia, bakeries, discos, butcher shops and internet cafes ringed the harbour.

Hydra has wisely outlawed motor vehicles on land, yet business still has to be done. The Greeks compensate magnificently, creating a system that blends nineteenth and twenty-first century technology. Motorised boats pulled into the quay. Forty two donkeys stood at the ready. Those merchants who could not afford four legged transport, used large two wheeled carts, pushing their goods ship to shore. This was the best show in town. Teams of donkeys carried everything, from steel bars to concrete sacks, stoves, smallish refrigerators, suitcases and gaily dressed tourists, up the valley walls. By 12 noon, hundreds of Greeks and *xeni* (foreigners) milled about, further adding to the absolute excitement and perfect confusion. Yet peace and quiet lay just around the next cove.

From the harbour, I followed the goat track that rose high along the cliffs. The fresh sea breeze carried the salt-laden air, enriching my lungs. The sea sparkled below the grey-stone cliffs, illuminating cerulean waters, transforming them into silver and gold. Pine trees grew into forests and prospered. After a short two kilometres, my path dropped down into the 19th century seaport hamlet of **Vlyhos** (Βλυχός), with two tavernas, one cliff top ouzerie, a small pebble beach, several *domatia* and a small harbour butting up onto the sea. Again, no motorised transport existed. Everything made its way by fishing caique or by sure-footed donkey.

Watching elderly fishermen repair their nets, I dined at the local taverna and enjoyed a succulent gyros of roast lamb and a glass of *hima*, the local wine. I promised myself that someday I would return to visit Vlyhos, a paradise by the sea.

I walked back past Hydra town and up the one hundred and forty two stairs to my mountain eerie. My balcony jutted out over the valley. I sat on the edge of the parapet. Far, far below, I could just make out the port. The burning embers of the fading Greek sun blazed through my canopy of star jasmine. Its flowers warmed gently, giving off a delicate perfume. A breeze swept down from the top of the hill. Somewhere, the rooster crowed again. I heard Pavarotti happily munching some of the purple nettles beneath my window. From the top of the crest high above my room, I could just barely hear the tinkling of goats bells, before drifting off into reverie.

Ed. Symphony is of course a Greek word (Συμφωνία) meaning also agreement from συμπνοια - harmony, concord and φωνή - voice.

Greek Food & Cooking

Shop 'til You Drop! *by Janet Ellis*

"Is that it? Only I can't carry much more", says Peter, who by now is carrying up to three bags in each hand, not to mention a full day-sac on his back.

We are on one of our shopping sprees, some 60 miles from home, in and around the Green Lanes area in North London. Here I am able to indulge in a different type of retail therapy from the type most women are associated with. The bags Peter is carrying are not full of shoes, clothes, make-up, etc but contain fruits, vegetables, meats and assorted groceries. So why do we travel so far from home when there is a perfectly good supermarket nearby loaded with food?

Well it's not just any food Peter is carrying, it's 'Greek food'. The big attraction of this area is the variety of shops, run mostly by Greek and Turkish Cypriots, full of goods we rarely see outside Greece. The area around Green Lanes is untidy and densely populated, and best visited during daylight. Green Lanes itself is a wide busy road with cars and buses continually running up and down, yet we are still able to smell the fresh produce, savour the aroma from the bakeries and hear the banter between shopkeeper and shopper, which makes for a great shopping experience.

We do this trip about four times a year and have now built up a routine to incorporate our favourite shops, starting with a grocers, just off Green Lanes, where we can park outside. Here we purchase all the heavy bulky items, such as 3 and 5 litre cans of extra virgin olive oil (we usually buy 3 or 4 of these, and at under £8 for 3 litres this is excellent value for money in the UK), small drums of olives, wines, feta, honey, kritharaki pasta, and more. We are now known here and our custom is usually rewarded with a discount on the wines, which of course we much appreciate. From here we head off on foot to Green Lanes to a greengrocers, which has an amazing display spilling out onto the pave-ment. When we arrive, just after 9 am, everything is beautifully presented and I very carefully select from the neatly arranged display, trying hard not to spoil the whole effect and cause an avalanche in the process! Here I can, depending on the season, pick up tiny sweet sultana grapes, quinces, broad beans (as

early as December), horta, kolokassi, ridge cucumbers, fresh vine leaves, round and flat beans, dates on the vine, figs, bunches of fresh herbs, good old fashioned dirty celery and more. Wonderful.

It's a short walk on to the butchers. Busy here on a Saturday morning. I am usually served by a short dumpy butcher with a glowing round face, he greets me with *"Hallo darleeen"* in his Greek accent. I have a far wider choice of meats here than those available from my local butcher, including goat, boiling fowl (anything up to 7lbs in weight), rabbits (these are complete with the pluck, have a sash round their middle, a metal clip of authenticity in the flesh – are rather expensive - and worth every penny), loukanika and highly spiced sausages, etc. He also sells sheep heads and various parts of a male pigs anatomy – use your imagination! To date I have not purchased either of these two but who knows, maybe one day, when I find the right recipes. All my purchases here are piled into Peter's day-sac, on one trip this was so loaded that the boiling fowls feet ended up protruding out of the top.

Just a bit further on we dip into two mini markets for graviera cheese, filo pastry, local yoghurt and anything else that takes my eye - maybe just a little more meat, maybe a different type of olive. The second of these two shops is quite an experience. It is very very busy, everyone is stocking up for the weekend and their baskets (they usually have more than one each) are brimming. The cash-out area is chaotic, it just has to be seen to be believed, people shuffling baskets along the floor in the queue and old ladies struggling out through the door with more carriers than they can comfortably carry. If you are going into the shop and you see one of these ladies coming at you, stand well back because believe me nothing stops them. And in case you were wondering if it's Peter who does all the carrying and why don't I invest in a donkey, then be assured it is now my turn to have my day sac filled, I have to keep my hands free of course, to carry the purse.

... And this is where we came in *"Is that it?......"*. Well no it isn't. We just have the bakery over the road and the 'pot shop', near where the car is parked, to visit. The window, of the bakery we favour, is decked out with sample wedding cakes, each a work of art in its own right and very Greek. As well as plain and olive breads we treat ourselves to some of their gorgeous honey soaked pastries to indulge in later on in the evening. Oh, by the way, I carry these - my purse is getting lighter now.

Finally, the pot shop. Anyone who read my piece in The Greek-o-File Vol. 2 about Peter's vegetable garden will know what I am talking about. This is the shop which sells everything from pots to statues to donkey saddles. So if one day I do get that donkey at least I know where to get a saddle, so that it can carry me and the shopping. Although we think we have bought

everything by now we usually find something - sweet lemons, an earthenware dish and they do sell the most wonderful green queen olives.

So that's it. We try to get done in about two hours so we can hopefully get back round the M25 (alias the Magic Roundabout) and home before lunch. On occasions we have still been in Green Lanes around lunchtime, usually when we have been to Trehantiri to buy some more music CD's, and we then treat ourselves to lunch at one of the many small restaurants. The most we have paid here is £7.60 for lamb with beans and stuffed aubergines, real value for money.

Back at home, Peter takes a well earned break and a snooze in his chair in the lounge, and I set to putting everything away and planning what I am going to cook - *Spetsofai* with the spicy sausages and some of the peppers - *kleftiko* with the goat - *stifado* with the rabbit - *koukia me to lathi* with the broad beans, yoghurt and dill - *tzatziki* with the ridge cucumbers and yoghurt - and so on.

I can't wait to start - this is where the fun begins.

Oh, just one afterthought. Last time Peter spotted whole lambs for sale in a butchers' window. Very reasonable they were too. What's that you said? - *"What the heck is she going to do with a whole lamb?"* No problem, they sell BBQ's in Green Lanes specially designed to spit roast whole lambs. Now I wonder if Peter can carry a whole lamb, a BBQ and the shopping? No maybe not - so where can I get a donkey? ... perhaps I should try ebay!

With special thanks to Sylvia & Terry at Greek-o-File for recommending Green Lanes.

A Diamond (Wine) in the Rough *by Miles Lambert-Gócs*

I used to go from Virginia to Para Liquors in Queens, New York every few months and haul away cases of Greek wines I could not find closer to home. My greatest find at Para's was Johnny Ternas, a gregarious sales clerk who could never do enough to advise me, like the time he unscrewed the cap from a bottle of Cyprus Muscat and urged me with a confident *"Smell that!"* as he thrust the mouth of the bottle under my nose. I hardly had time for an inhalation before he recapped the bottle and stuck it in my shopping cart. But it was also Johnny who put me onto the scent of Siatista.

Johnny's parents were from western Macedonia, and Siatista was his mother's hometown. His praise for the place's sweet *liasto* wine was lavish and left me thinking that the 20-year-old vintage belongs among the world's consummate wine experiences. Being more a believer in the printed word, I stopped off at the Library of Congress in Washington, DC to check out Johnny's implausible story even before I got home to Virginia to unload my wines. I was amazed to find him borne out in the several exhaustive bibles about the Balkans written by early 19th century travellers. The Frenchman Ami Boué (1840) went so far as to list Siatista first in naming several places he thought deserved special mention for their wines. Siatista immediately became a *must* destination and on my next visit to Para's I pumped Johnny for more information. He heartily recommended that I visit the town and referred me to his Aunt Marigo there.

Siatista must have been the sort of place that gave rise to the Greek adage, 'a village that appears needs no guide'. The town was nowhere in sight and without road signs to point the way I almost despaired of finding it. While my map showed it lying between Grevena and Kozani, once I was actually on the ground, the overgrown fields and nearly barren mountain slopes along the road gave me no clue as to where an inhabited place might be. But my book learning by that time had informed me that Siatista is an old centre of the Macedonian fur trade and I got the 'guide' I needed when in the middle of nowhere I came across the Macedonian equivalent of a factory outlet store for furs. I took the next turn off the main road and passed first through a cleft in the mountains and then through the remnants of what once must have been the town gateway. At the top of the road stood Siatista.

Finding Johnny's Aunt Marigo was a snap. The first person I encountered knew her and pointed out her home. It was not at all far and sat behind a

little portal and courtyard.   But Siatista is not the Greece of stucco-and-whitewash Aegean cubes. Aunt Marigo's home was a very substantial one constructed for weather in which jackets are not put away until June and grapes are not harvested until well into October. My knock on the door produced Aunt Marigo herself, who struck me as a complete anachronism. Dressed in black workaday clothing with a regional cut to it, she spoke in such strongly dialectical Greek that all I understood was that she was in the middle of making cheese.

Aunt Marigo quickly handed me over to her son, Johnny's cousin, and went back to her curds and whey. Apparently on Johnny's past inculcation of English, the cousin introduced himself as 'Dzordz' (George). He did not look at all like Johnny, but his resemblance in manner was uncanny. Just like his American cousin, Dzordz came at me with a helpful familiarity that transcended the Greeks' usual probing hospitality, in slightly quirky ways. He immediately took me on a no-rooms-barred inspection tour of the premises, and as if saving the best for last we finished off at the bathroom, the elaborate plumbing of which Dzordz obviously expected me to find end-lessly fascinating.

I thought hydraulics might be his line, but when I asked him about his work he replied that it is furs. Every fall he would fill up his car with furs and head up through Yugoslavia to Hungary, Czechoslovakia and Poland to sell them off. In short order I found myself outside with Dzordz, the two of us peering into the engine of his Orient Express jalopy. Of course we also had to cram into the car and take the tour of Siatista, with occasional stops so that Dzordz could introduce *"a friend of Dzonni."*

Faded signs of one-time wealth were apparent everywhere along our way. The town had prospered from the fur trade with central Europe during Ottoman times and even became a scholastic centre on the financial strength of it. The same routes to central Europe known to Dzordz had been plied for generations on end going back to antiquity and Hellenic commercial interest in Baltic amber. Not even communism had managed to shut down the ancient routes, as demonstrated by Dzordz's car, which showed every bit of injury that communist Balkan roadways could inflict on democratic Greek vehicles.

When Dzordz and I finally returned to the starting gate we went directly to the only space in the house that we had not previously viewed, the wine 'cellar.' Actually, it was on the ground floor, off from the dining room. We found Aunt Marigo there, making her cheese. Behind her were three oak barrels of enormous size, relics of infinitely better days for Siatistan wine growers. I expected Dzordz to draw wine from one of the barrels but instead he reached down to a cubby-hole and pulled out a home-corked bottle. Back in the dining room he poured us a bit of its incipiently brownish red contents into two tumblers. The wine was a 15-year-old dry one in a condition that tweaks the nose of cosmopolitan professionals of the contemporary Greek wine industry.

Dzordz was in no hurry to move on to the sweet *liasto* wine he knew Johnny had sent me for. Instead he spoke at some length about his travels in central Europe and his ways of doing business there while circumventing communist red-tape. But when I brought him back to wine and *liasto* he described Siatistan cellar practices in more detail than he had the bathroom plumbing. *Liasto* literally means 'sunned' and refers to the fact that the grapes are dried a bit to increase sugar content before the wine making begins. It is made in much of Greece, but Dzordz mentioned the local peculiarity of separating the *liasto* grape-must from the grape-skins by filtering through a mesh of clean goat's wool. It made me wonder what I might be in for.

The household's *liasto* was resting in a small chestnut cask in the cellar. As soon as Aunt Marigo saw Dzordz come to draw some she abandoned the cheese and rushed into the dining room to replace our tumblers with stemware glasses Dzordz had brought back from Poland or Czechoslovakia or Hungary. Dzordz then poured the amberish liquid.

Its bouquet was possessed of singular aromatic nuances and was also distinguished by an aromatic lightness that swiftly and softly penetrated the nasal passages up to the 'upper register' of smell sensors. While as an objective wine reporter I prudently had to remain dubious about the role of the goat's wool in this paragon of old-time wine making, I had no doubt that Siatista's Liasto was the best thing Johnny Ternas ever pushed under my nose.

Adapted extract from Miles' book 'Greek Salad' - see Book Reviews.

Greek Olives *by Sylvia Cook*

When I first sampled olives as a teenager, I hated them. On early adult holidays abroad to Spain I tried again - but those hard green bitter Spanish olives did nothing for me. I didn't try again for many years, until one day in Greece I sampled a Kalamata olive ... mmmm! This was more to my liking. Since then I've happily eaten Greek olives of all kinds - black, occasionally green and all those purple, red and brown shades between. Probably the succulent firm shiny Kalamata olive remains my favourite.

The olive has been a staple of the Greek diet for thousands of years. I often wonder how they first found that the bitter hard fruit of the olive tree could be made more palatable by curing, or that when crushed it would yield an oil with so many healthy uses. Olives were the gift (of most value) of the goddess Athena which won her the competition with Poseidon for supremacy over the people of Athens. Olives and olive oil are known to have been used since early Minoan times in Crete 3500BC. An olive branch symbolising peace was awarded to winners at the ancient Olympic Games from the first ones in 776BC and later huge quantities of olive oil were the prize for winners at the Panathenaic Games. Its value has never been disputed.

Although olive presses are now mechanical, there is not a lot that modern technology can do to simplify the olive harvest. Harvest time is from October to December, varying depending on location and the kind of use the olives will be put to - earlier when plump and green or just turning colour for table olives, later when fully ripened and shiny black for oil. As harvest time approaches, black nets or sheets of plastic are usually laid below the olive trees to catch the ripe olives that fall from the branches and those that are encouraged to fall by shaking the branches or beating them with sticks. Separating the olives from the debris is tiring work too - either by winnowing (throwing sheetfuls up into the air for the wind to blow away the leaves) or 'sifting' through chicken wire on a frame at table height onto fine nets below. The best method to prevent bruising is to pick by hand, often cutting off branches to handle at ground level. Olives on one tree will not all ripen together, so trees need to be revisited.

I have heard harvesting rates from 1 tree per person per day to 7 trees per day, perhaps varying based on fitness and practice, or maybe size and variety of tree. Certainly there seem to be different cultivation methods and varieties. Trees cut back to grow only low branches must be easier for picking than towering olive groves. You need to get the olives to the local olive press quickly to ensure they do not start to ferment in the heat they create. If you own an olive grove and don't feel fit enough to harvest all your own, you can hire olive pickers, often Albanians familiar with olive cultivation. They may be paid with half of the harvest in oil rather than in money.

4 to 5 kilos of olives will yield one kilo of oil, each tree up to 10 litres in a good year - the first pressing being the best extra virgin quality. Trees will often only produce high yields in alternate years.

Again regional methods vary, but to prepare olives for the table you need to remove the bitterness, then cure and mature the olives, usually with salt. Commercially the first stage is often speeded up by rinsing in 'lye' or soda, an alkaline solution to remove the bitterness in days rather than months, but probably the natural methods are best producing mature eating olives by spring, which should keep in sealed airtight containers up to 18 months. Olives in brine will need to be refrigerated once the seal is broken, but in olive oil a cool cupboard should be fine for a while. In some areas dry salting is an alternative method for preserving olives.

We have eaten interesting 'dry' tasting olives early in autumn shortly after picking. They were slit with a knife then rinsed daily and left in fresh water for one week then in salt water for a week or two. The best home produced olives we had were picked mid December (in Lesvos) when they were rosy pink and yellowy green like miniature ripe apples. First rinsed then popped uncut into a 1.5 litre fizzy drink bottle, filled with water, a piled teaspoon of salt added and the lid firmly screwed down. The bottle was turned every few days (we had to unscrew the top to let excess gas out once or twice

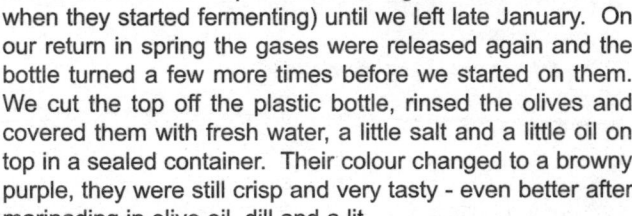

when they started fermenting) until we left late January. On our return in spring the gases were released again and the bottle turned a few more times before we started on them. We cut the top off the plastic bottle, rinsed the olives and covered them with fresh water, a little salt and a little oil on top in a sealed container. Their colour changed to a browny purple, they were still crisp and very tasty - even better after marinading in olive oil, dill and a little lemon juice.

Other marinade ingredients to try include garlic, chopped parsley, chopped preserved lemons, wine vinegar instead of lemon juice or how about spicy olives in oil, coriander, garlic and chilli or black pepper.

Koukia Me to Lathi - Broad Beans with Oil *by Janet Ellis*

Broad Beans are a little like cats – you either love or hate them! Me - I love them, so I can't go wrong in Greece, where there are plenty of both. If you like broad beans (you don't have to like cats as well) you will probably enjoy this recipe.

Young tender shelled broad beans are best for this recipe, or the whole pod before the beans have developed to any size inside.

500g fresh broad beans or whole pods

olive oil

2-3 shallots, finely chopped

1 clove of garlic, crushed

1 tblsp chopped fresh dill

250g (apprx) tub of Greek yoghurt

salt and pepper

Method

☐ Boil the beans in salted water until tender - fresh young shelled beans about 5 mins, shop bought (usually older) 15-20 mins, complete young pods 10-15 mins.

☐ Drain the beans and if you have used older beans and the skins are tough remove and discard these, retaining just the inside beans.

☐ Sweat the finely chopped shallots and crushed garlic in a little olive oil until soft.

☐ Add the drained beans and warm through.

☐ Stir in the chopped dill and yoghurt and warm through again, without boiling.

☐ Season to taste and serve.

Any leftovers can be kept and eaten cold as a salad.

Spetsofai - Casserole of Sausage & Peppers *by Janet Ellis*

It was in early May and our holiday was nearing the end before we discovered a great taverna just off the square in Naxos town. *"Tell us what you like"*, we were told, *"and we will cook it for you for tomorrow night."* Spetsofai was Peter's choice and he was not disappointed - bangers yes, but cooked in a rich Greek tomato sauce with peppers, this was a memorable dish.

650-700g mixed long peppers

Olive oil

500g spicy Greek or spicy butcher's sausages*

2 onions, sliced

2 garlic cloves, crushed

500g skinned roughly chopped fresh tomatoes (or 1 400g tin)

1 tblsp concentrated tomato puree (leave out if tinned tomatoes used)

150ml hot water

1 tsp oregano

salt and pepper

Method

- ☐ Cut the peppers in half lengthways and remove the seeds.
- ☐ Fry them in an ovenproof pan or casserole, in olive oil, until they start to turn brown, remove and drain on kitchen paper.
- ☐ Next prick the sausages and fry them in the same pan, just long enough to brown on the outside, then remove from the pan.
- ☐ Add a little more oil, if necessary, and fry the sliced onions and crushed garlic, until soft.
- ☐ Add the tomatoes to the onions and garlic and cook for a few minutes.
- ☐ Return the sausages and peppers to the pan.
- ☐ Mix the tomato puree with the water and pour over the sausages etc.
- ☐ Finally sprinkle over the oregano and season with salt and pepper.
- ☐ Put the lid on the pan or casserole and place in a preheated oven at Gas 4/ 180°C for about 1 hour.
- ☐ At the end of the cooking time, if necessary, you may like to remove the peppers and sausages and keep them warm while you reduce the remaining sauce, until thickened.

> ** I've also used Budgen's Mexican sausages successfully.*
> *Adjust garlic, oregano, etc to suit spiciness of sausages and to taste.*

Fakes (Φακές) - Lentil Soup by Sylvia Cook

Dried lentils and beans are the traditional winter staple diet of many Greek villagers and this is a real winter warmer - nutritious and tasty. One great advantage of lentils is that unlike other dried pulses, they do not need to be soaked overnight before cooking.

8 oz / 250 g green or brown lentils
1 medium onion, quartered & sliced
1 stick celery, finely sliced
1 carrot, halved & finely sliced
4 tblsp olive oil
2 garlic cloves
1 tin chopped tomatoes
1 tblsp tomato puree
2 bay leaves
1 tblsp oregano
1 tblsp wine vinegar (optional)
salt & black pepper
1.5 pints/ 1 litre chicken or vegetable stock (or water)
Chopped fresh parsley to serve.

Method

❑ Rinse lentils and generously cover with water in a large saucepan. Bring to boil. After 5 minutes drain lentils, discarding the water.

❑ Meanwhile gently cook sliced onions in olive oil, add celery and carrot slices. Sauté until soft (about 5 minutes).

❑ Add crushed garlic, tomatoes, tomato puree, bay leaves, oregano and pepper, lentils & stock. Heat to simmering point. Do NOT add salt until cooking is complete as it inhibits softening of the lentils.

❑ Simmer all together for 30-40 minutes, or until lentils are soft.

❑ Add salt and wine vinegar to taste. Serve sprinkled with chopped fresh parsley (flat preferably) if available and fresh crusty bread.

 © Greek-o-File™ Vol. 3

Chicken in Avgolemono Sauce *by Rosemary Barron*

Offered to Greek-o-File from her book 'Flavours of Greece' (see p159 reviews).

The taste of this classic springtime dish is fresh and clean, the flavours light and fragrant: zesty lemon, delicate dill, and mild vitamin-rich lettuce. Serve with Potatoes in a Clay Pot or boiled new potatoes and a dry white wine to enhance the subtle flavour. (Serves 4)

1.6kg/3.5lb chicken, cut into serving pieces, skin & excess fat removed.
450ml/16 fl oz Chicken stock or water
2 carrots, cut into large pieces
1 stick celery, cut into large pieces
3 bay leaves
6 black peppercorns
6 spring onions, trimmed, with 5cm/2inches green left intact
2 tblsp extra virgin olive oil
2 heads Cos or endive lettuce, trimmed of outer leaves & tough
*   stems, cut into 6mm/ ¼ inch ribbons*
1 small bunch fresh dill, coarsely chopped
Sea salt and freshly ground white pepper to taste
Juice of 2 large lemons
3 eggs separated

❑ Combine the chicken, stock, carrots, celery, bay leaves and pepper-corns in a large heavy saucepan. Slowly brong to boil, cover, reduce the heat and simmer 40 minutes or until the chicken is tender.

❑ Meanwhile, slice the spring onions lengthways in half and cut into 2.5cm/ 1 inch long pieces. Warm the olive oil in a heavy sauté pan and cook the spring onions over low heat until soft, about 2 minutes. Add the lettuce, cover and cook, stirring once or twice until wilted, about 2 minutes. Stir in the dill, salt and pepper and half the lemon juice. Add the cooked chicken to the pan and set aside.

❑ Strain the cooking broth into a bowl. Whisk the egg whites in a large bowl with a whisk or an electric mixer until they hold soft peaks. Add the yolks and whisk 1 minute longer. Slowly add the remaining lemon juice and the broth, whisking constantly. Transfer to a medium sauce-pan and gently heat over low heat, stirring constantly with a wooden spoon, until creamy and slightly thickened, about 5 minutes; don't let the sauce boil.

❑ Pour the sauce over the chicken, place the sauté pan over low heat and heat to warm through - do not boil. Season to taste, transfer to a warm serving dish and serve at once.

Syka (Σύκα) Figs *by Sylvia Cook*

Figs ripen abundantly in most parts of Greece from August to September. This is the time to eat figs at their best - fresh off the tree, washed and with no adornment. Usually they ripen in such large quantities that anyone who owns a fig tree is giving them away to friends and neighbours, and preserving the rest. Some will be made into fig jam or preserved whole in syrup, but most are simply dried, their natural sugars being sufficient to keep them for a long time. They will be laid out carefully to dry in the sun on a raised frame of bamboo or reeds, sometimes finished off in a very low oven, then the best are packed carefully in boxes in layers, with bay leaves and maybe other herbs between. They make ideal gifts.

If you have been the recipient of one of these gifts, you may have wondered what to do with your dried figs once back home. Here are some simple ideas, starting with my favourite.

◇ Sit figs closely together on the base of a flat dish with stalk upwards. Pour sweet red wine (perhaps Mavrodaphne) or Metaxa and orange juice (50/50) over the figs to about half centimetre/ ¼ inch deep, cover with cling film and leave at least 3 days (they will keep and improve if left weeks or even months). Top up if the liquid is all absorbed. To serve, transfer the number required to a fresh dish, warm through in the oven or microwave and serve with creamy Greek yoghurt.

◇ For occasional snacks or after a meal, moist dried figs must be better for you than chocolate bars, biscuits or puddings. Warming them briefly in a microwave or oven will help them plump out and enhance their flavour.

◇ Slit figs at top and insert either a half or quarter walnut or an almond inside each and place in a flat ovenproof dish. Melt a tablespoon of honey in 3 tablespoons of water in a saucepan with a cinnamon stick and a few slivers of lemon peel. Pour over the figs and cook in a moderate oven (Gas 4/ 180°C) for 20 minutes. Remove lemon & cinnamon and serve with Greek yoghurt or vanilla ice cream.

◇ Add a fig or two per person to the roasting tray with slow roast (covered) chicken, lamb or pork. The figs absorb the meat juices and taste quite delicious.

◇ Chop figs in pieces and use in any recipe in place of, or mixed with dried fruits :
   - muesli for breakfast
   - cake mixes
   - bread dough.

Xenophon & The March of the Ten Thousand
by Terry Cook

There was a man in the army named Xenophon, an Athenian, who was neither general nor captain nor private, but had accompanied the expedition because Proxenus, an old friend of his, had sent him an invitation to go with him, promising him that, if he would go, he would make him a friend of Cyrus, whom he regarded as more worthy than any in his own country.

ΞΕΝΟΦΩΝ

That is how Xenophon introduced himself in the story of the 400 BC version of the 'Grand old Duke of York'. In excess of ten thousand mercenary soldiers marched over a thousand miles from home, deep into foreign territory 'up the hill' to Central Persia, where they were left high and dry without leaders. Xenophon - adventurer, opportunist, bored playboy fed up with the political and social scene of Athens, jumped at the chance to join them, little knowing it would fall to him to 'march them down again' to the safety of their homeland. Whether he saw it as a future book *(he wrote the Anabasis 20 years later describing the whole 2 year excursion in intricate detail)*, or whether he was just looking for some new excitement in his life, we are not told.

Indeed, some commentators feel his journalistic style was too romantic and a very biased view of events, written with the 'best seller' list in mind, and not as a dedicated historian just recording the facts. But then, the whole affair was a little embarrassing and somewhat inglorious for the Greek audience of that time. It was the twilight years of the Golden Age of Ancient Greece, the days of philosophers, of advances in knowledge of science, medicine and understanding of the world around us. Great dramas were enacted in the theatres of Greece, but Athens had lost the power struggle of the city states to Sparta and there was great unrest politically, despite advancing democracy.

There was also a looming social problem in the form of many veteran soldiers who had spent three decades fighting in the Peloponnesian Wars, now faced with no homes, no families and no work or means of living. Persia had long been a major player in Greek fortunes, and now the antagonism between the two heirs of the Persian King, Darius, led to plot and counter plot in which these 13,000 Greek soldiers became entangled. Prince Cyrus the younger son sought to build an army on the pretence of subduing the

Pisidians, a troublesome bunch in Asia Minor, and longtime adversaries of the Greeks.

He easily recruited thousands of displaced fighting men, probably more eager for the promised fortune than the honour of fighting for a foreign leader, even though the Spartans owed much to Persia for help in conquering Athens. One of the generals thus enlisted was an old buddy of Xenophon, and perhaps to ensure some good companionship and relief from the stress of warmongering, or maybe knowing how disillusioned Xenophon was with life in Athens, Proxenus wrote a letter imploring him to pack his bags and join him for the experience of a lifetime!

Xenophon, now in his thirties, saw the opportunity but was not at first convinced that it was a good idea. He had been an ardent student of the great Socrates, and still admired him and valued his opinion on just about everything. *"What should I do?"* he asked his mentor, hoping for some encouragement to venture forth and sample new horizons. Socrates seemed somewhat hesitant in giving his blessing. Not wanting to appear too disapproving, he suggested his eager disciple should seek the advice of the Delphic oracle.

This was not exactly what he wanted to hear, so Xenophon laid his own interpretation on the master's wisdom, and asked the oracle to which gods he should sacrifice in order to secure a successful outcome for his plan. Apollo, the voice of Delphic wisdom, told him to honour Zeus Soter, but when Xenophon told Socrates, he was 'not well pleased'. However, he realised the strong-willed young man had clearly set his heart on going, so bade him do as instructed, albeit fearing for the attitude of the Athenian authorities towards him openly assisting a professed enemy of the state.

Taking the next available ship across the Aegean, Xenophon caught up with his compatriots and the march uphill from Sardis near the coast of Asia Minor deep into the interior of Persia began. It is recorded that only one commander knew the real plans of Cyrus, but it wasn't too long before other generals and soldiers alike suspected something 'fishy' from the distance and direction they were headed. It took all of Clearchus' powers of persuasion and promises of high financial rewards to keep the army from deserting in large numbers. Finally, far too distant from the sea for the Greeks' comfort, Cyrus joined battle with his brother's forces at Cunaxa not far from current Baghdad. Unfortunately his campaign met an abrupt end with his death.

Confusion gave way to disarray, amid talks of armistice and safe conduct out of alien territory. But lies and deceit led the Greek generals into a trap where they were all slaughtered, leaving thousands of poorly armed soldiers and all their camp followers as sitting targets for a reprisal massacre by Ataxerxes, the victorious Persian leader. Probably more from a sense of self-preservation than military training, Xenophon - after a dream which con-

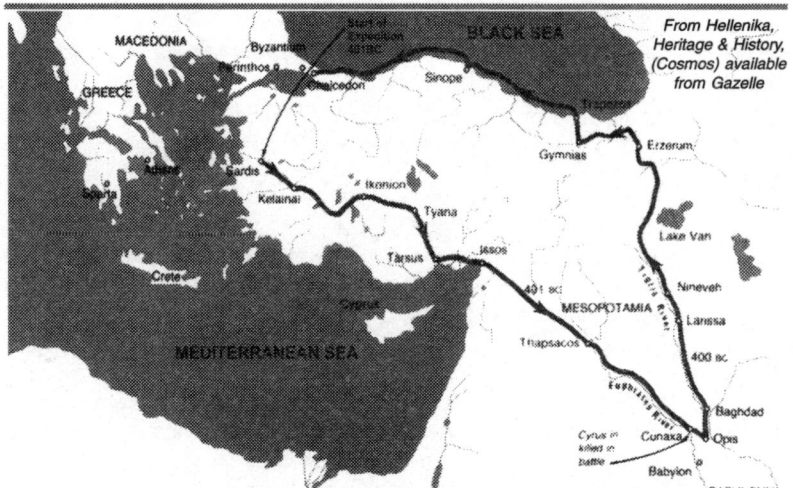

From Hellenika, Heritage & History, (Cosmos) available from Gazelle

centrated his mind on the situation - became the champion of the army with his clear plan to march north to the Black Sea. Wary of help offered by the commander of the Persian forces, because of his obvious treachery, Xenophon rallied the Greeks to begin a hazardous trip through Kurdistan, Armenia and the surrounding mountainous terrain to the security of Greek colonies on the Black Sea coast.

Skill and determination, fighting off local tribes and foraging for food through a bleak winter, led to the successful achievement of his aims. After five months 8,600 men reached the Greek colony of Trapezos from where they travelled back home by sea. Xenophon eventually reached the shores of the Peloponnese to find Socrates had drunk hemlock and died after Athens' rejection of his teachings. Xenophon, preferring the Spartan philosophy, fought with them against Athens and Thebes. He was banished from Athens, but his new allies gave him an estate at Skillos near Olympia, where he devoted his time to writing, horsemanship and sport. His works included a continuation of the contemporary history started by Thucidides, a romantic biography of Cyrus the Great and an apology for Socrates as well as other treatises on subjects close to his heart.

In 371 BC Sparta was defeated in battle by the Elians, who promptly ejected Xenophon from their land, but since Sparta and Athens had become allies again, his exile was revoked by Athens. It appears however, that his final days were spent around Corinth, where he continued writing well into his eighties and left us a wealth of literature on many themes, which, if not always historically accurate, are an intriguing personal insight into the life and times, the turmoils and hardships of that period of Greek history.

Ancient Greek Architecture *by Mary Lambell*

One of the joys of visiting Greece in modern times, is being able to see remnants of ancient buildings erected 2,000 to 3,000 years ago when the ancient Greek civilisation was at its height. Most of the structures from ancient Greece which are still in existence today are temples and theatres.

Other public buildings like treasuries (as at Delphi), or stoas (colonnades) usually employed the same techniques and style of architecture as temples. It should be remembered that the Greeks used no cement to hold the stones together. Metal clamps were used, (iron coated in lead); and the basic structural system was the 'post and lintel'. This meant that the roof span of a building was limited, or that internal columns were used to support the roof. Even with these constraints, or perhaps because of them, Greek architects built structures which were both impressive and elegant, and have been copied by later generations throughout the world.

Greek Temples

Every Greek city had numerous temples to accommodate the many gods. In addition there were sacred sites dedicated mainly to one deity, like Olympia or Delphi. The temple housed the statue of the god. Worship, in the form of prayer and sacrifice, took place outside where the altar stood.

A typical Greek temple comprised the *naos,* the inner room, facing east and housing the cult statue, which stood on a raised platform called the *stylobate,* surrounded by two or three steps; the entrance porch, the *pronaos*, contained columns, usually two, sometimes four or more. For the sake of symmetry the temple often had an *opisthodomos,* back porch, even if there was no door. Surrounding the naos was nearly always a colonnade, the *peristylion*. The normal number of columns was six by thirteen, but this was not a hard and fast rule.

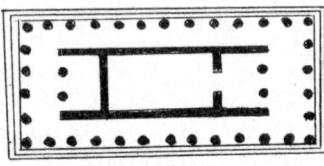

Plan of Temple of Hephaistos

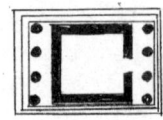

Plan of Temple of Athene Nike

The Greeks used two main orders of architecture, *Doric* and *Ionic*.

The Doric Order

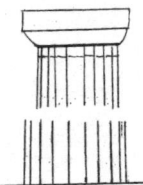

The Doric order is the simplest and most temples in mainland Greece were in this form. Ironically South Italy and Sicily have some of the best examples, but a good, well-preserved example is the *Temple of Hephaistos* in the Athenian Agora. It is the columns and the entablature (the section above the columns), which distinguish the orders.

A Doric column has no base: it rests on the floor and has 20 flutes, which are sharp-edged. The capital consists of two parts, the rounded *echinus* and the square *abacus*. The height of the column is 4-6 times the diameter of the base (as a general rule the earlier the temple the greater the relative thickness of the columns). Above is the *architrave*, a plain band of stone made from sections which join in the centre of each column capital. Above this is the *frieze*, made up of alternating *triglyphs* (vertical carvings resembling the Roman numeral III) and *metopes* (square blocks often containing relief sculpture). At each end of the temple the *pediment* (gable end), usually contained sculpture, either relief or freestanding.

As well as the Temple of Hephaistos, there are many other Doric examples you can see today:

- Temple of Apollo, Corinth (an early, 6th century BC, example in what is now mainly a Roman city).

- Temple of Hera, Olympia (columns vary as they gradually replaced the earlier wooden ones).

- Temple of Aphaia, Aegina (a good example here of an internal colonnade of two-tier columns to support the roof).

- Temple of Apollo, Delphi (a spectacular setting, home of the Oracle).

- Temple of Poseidon, Sounion (another spectacular setting on the cliff top, appropriate for the sea god visible to homecoming sailors).

Doric, Temple of Hephaistos, Athens

The Ionic Order

This order is derived from the Ionian Greeks in Asia Minor and is more common there and on the Aegean islands. Only two such temples can now be seen on the mainland: the *Temple of Athena Nike* and the *Erechtheion*, (which is unconventional in many respects), both on the Athenian Acropolis. The Ionic order is much more delicate and elegant in its detail, and was used in a more flexible way, but there are basic features to distinguish it
from the Doric. The column has a moulded base, 24 flutes which are flat-edged, and in height is 8-12 times the diameter of the base. This makes it appear more slim and elegant. The capital comprises *volutes,* scroll-like carvings, topped with a thin square *abacus.* The *architrave* consists of three horizontal bands of stone, each projecting slightly outwards over the one below. The *frieze* here is a continuous band of relief sculpture, and the *pediment* is generally left empty. The column base, the volutes and other parts of the structure usually contain a great deal of detailed carving, known as *mouldings.*

On both orders the architectural and sculptural details would have been painted in bright colours, and there would be extra decoration in bronze, gold or silver.

An Ionic example you can see today is the Temple of Hera, Samos (double row of columns in *peristylion,* some columns unfluted, not much left standing).

The *Parthenon* is basically a Doric temple, larger than usual, but with an additional Ionic feature, the continuous frieze round the *naos.* It was from this frieze, that a large part was sadly removed by Lord Elgin, and is currently (2004) housed in the British Museum.

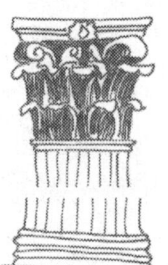

The Corinthian Order

A third order, the *Corinthian,* came later. It resembles the Ionic order but has more elaborate capitals, based on the acanthus plant. An example is the huge Temple of Olympian Zeus in Athens, which was finally completed by
the Roman Emperor Hadrian in the second century AD. This order was much more popular with the Romans.

Corinthian, Temple of Olympian Zeus

Constantinople 1204 *by Jonathan Harris*

In June 1203 the inhabitants of Constantinople, the capital of the Byzantine empire, crowded onto their ramparts to witness an ominous sight. In the waters of the Bosphoros, which lapped against the city walls, hundred of ships lay at anchor, manned by thousands of formidably armed knights and foot soldiers. This was the fleet of the Fourth Crusade, under the command of the Doge of Venice, Enrico Dandolo and a number of French nobles. Originally destined to sail to Egypt, to fight against the Muslims there and ultimately to recover Jerusalem, the fleet had changed course for Constantinople when a Byzantine prince, Alexios Angelos, persuaded its leaders to intervene in a dynastic power struggle. Alexios' father, the emperor Isaac II, had been deposed by his brother, Alexios' uncle, and now languished in a dungeon beneath the imperial palace.

Powerful though the fleet was, it should not necessarily have posed a threat. Constantinople was guarded on all sides by the strongest fortifications that could be devised and had never been captured by a foreign army, in spite of numerous attempts over the centuries. The usurper therefore felt confident to defy the crusaders and refused to restore Isaac II to the throne. This time, however, the defence went badly wrong. The attacking crusaders succeeded in breaking the chain which guarded entry to Constantinople's harbour, the Golden Horn, thus giving them access to the spot where the walls were weakest. Sensing defeat, the usurper fled. Isaac II found himself emperor once more, though real power was in the hands of his co-emperor, his son Alexios.

That should have been the end of the matter but the crusaders now demanded to be paid. In a rash moment, Alexios had promised them 200,000 silver marks in return for their help and he soon discovered that the imperial treasury was empty. To raise this enormous sum, he had no choice but to tax his subjects heavily and to seize church treasures to melt down into coin. Not surprisingly, these actions aroused intense resentment amongst the people of Constantinople and in January 1204, Alexios was overthrown and murdered in a palace coup. Furious at this turn of events and apprehensive that they might never get their money, the crusaders decided to attack. The first assault against the walls along the Golden Horn on 9 April was

Design by Nigel Bradley from
'Byzantium and the Crusades'

repulsed but five days later the crusaders returned to the fray. This time they succeeded in using scaling ladders to gain a foothold on top of the walls and in opening up a breach through which the main body of the army could pour into the city.

What happened next was shocking, even in an age more accustomed to the savagery of war than ours. Constantinople was a Christian city, and the crusaders had all taken a vow to fight for the faith against nonbelievers. Yet once they were inside the city they behaved with a barbarity which led one Byzantine to comment that the Constantinopolitans would have received better treatment if their city had been taken by the Saracens.

Most of the crusaders were from small villages and had never seen anything like the wealth and sophistication of an Eastern Mediterranean city like Constantinople. Once resistance was at an end they gave themselves over to frenzied looting, one crusader exulting that *"gold and silver, table services and precious stones, satin and silk, mantles of squirrel fur, ermine and miniver and every choicest thing to be found on this earth"* were grabbed as booty. Many incidents of rape were recorded. One eyewitness saw a young girl being dragged away by a French soldier: her elderly father pursued them but could not keep up and fell exhausted into the mud. In the general confusion, fires broke out and large areas of Constantinople were reduced to ashes.

Not even churches were spared. A crowd of crusaders entered the cathedral of Hagia Sophia, some of them not even bothering to dismount from their horses, and started to remove the gold and silver candlesticks and ecclesiastical vessels. So abundant and heavy was the plunder that they brought in donkeys to carry it all away. Nor were clergymen averse to joining in the feeding frenzy. At the monastery of Christ Pantokrator, the looters were led by a German abbot. He grabbed all the relics of the saints that he could find and departed with them hidden in his cassock. Such behaviour was seen as justified because the Byzantine Church was in schism with that of the West, the major issues being the refusal of the Byzantines to accept the authority of the pope and the wording of the Latin Creed. Much of the loot disappeared forever, but some can still be seen in the treasuries of cathedrals the length and breadth of Europe, such as the Byzantine reliquary at Limburg in Germany, which no doubt travelled in the saddle bag of a returning knight. Most famous of all are the four bronze horses which grace the faŋade of the church of St. Mark in Venice, which were taken from the hippodrome in Constantinople.

The success of the crusaders in 1204 was short-lived. Although they set up an emperor of their own to replace the Byzantine emperor, they were unable to establish themselves permanently. After fifty-seven years of inept rule, they were ejected from Constantinople by the Byzantines in 1261. Nevertheless, the damage had been done. A fatal blow had been struck against the Byzantine empire and in its weakened state it proved unable to resist the growing power of the Ottoman Turks to the East. In 1453 Constantinople was captured a second time, by the Ottoman Sultan Mehmed II, and this time the loss was permanent.

Another enduring legacy of the Fourth Crusade was its effect on the Greek view of the West. The shock and outrage caused by the sack of Constantinople ensured that the schism between the Churches would be never be healed so that it still exists today in the division between the Orthodox and Catholic Churches. Moreover, the betrayal of 1204 can still provoke powerful emotions in Greece. When Pope John-Paul II visited Athens in 2001, he felt compelled to apologise publicly for the excesses of the crusaders even though they were neither authorised nor encouraged by the papacy at the time, and there were many who would have preferred not to see the pope there at all. Although Greece is now firmly a member of the European Union, memories of the sack of Constantinople still influence the occasionally ambivalent attitude of some of her people towards the West.

Further Reading

Michael Angold, The Fourth Crusade (Longman 2003, ISBN 058 2356 105)

Jonathan Harris, Byzantium and the Crusades (Hambledon and London 2003, ISBN 185 2852 984)

John Julius Norwich, Byzantium: The Decline and Fall (Penguin 1995, ISBN 014 0114 491)

Jonathan Phillips, The Fourth Crusade and the Sack of Constantinople (Jonathan Cape 2004, ISBN 0224069861)

Note from Ed. *Although Constantinople is in Turkey and has been known as Istanbul since Ottoman times, the head of the Eastern Orthodox church is still based there and a small Greek population remains, as agreed in the Lausanne Treaty 1923.*

Pan - a God or the Devil? *by Terry Cook*

The ancient Greeks were well-known for 'inventing' a god for every eventuality of life covering all their requirements from the cradle to the grave, and beyond. Some of these deities were simply an attempt to explain what they saw around them, some to hang their hopes or fears on and some were even to justify what they did or felt. Whether it was actually the rough-living shepherds of Arcadia who were responsible for the 'emergence' of the god Pan or whether he really did exist from the very beginnings of all things, I leave the reader to decide. Whichever way we may see Pan today, it is a fact of recorded history that he was among the most influential and most worshipped of all the ***pan***-theon of the Greek Gods. Even there, you see his name – for some said he was called Pan (from παν the Greek word meaning ALL) because he was ALL things to ALL men and even ALL the gods of Olympus were impressed by him.

His origins are lost in the myth of time – some say he was born of Hermes and a nymph, or Penelope, or others that he was the seed of Zeus and Hybris. What is certain is that he first appeared in Arcadia, and was worshipped by all who made their living from the land or the woods or the animals. Indeed he was portrayed as having the body of a man but with horns sprouting from his forehead, a goat's beard and a crooked nose, pointed ears and the tail and feet of a goat. It is said he was so repulsive to look at that on first sight, his mother fled in disgust. Although later artists toned down his appearance, his image was used in mediaeval times to portray none less than the devil himself. Certainly his antics recorded in Greek Myth are devilish to say the least.

He loved to wander the forests of Arcadia, dancing and playing with the nymphs and the Satyrs, of whom some say he was the chief. He became a solid member of the Dionysus crowd, and we all know the sort of things that lot got up to! Having a good time was the name of the game - perhaps the way his early followers, whose life was hard and rough, justified letting their hair down to relax. But he also got the blame when the hunters had a bad day. They would curse and whip the wooden image they tended to have of Pan in their dwellings. He was supposed to be their patron and look after them - but even the gods had off days!

It was said that one thing he really could not tolerate was being disturbed from his slumbers - and being a hot climate, he often took a siesta during the middle of the day. When aroused by some careless traveller making too much noise, he would take his revenge by jumping out in their path and scaring them half to death. Our word 'panic' is said to come from this very habit of Pan revealing himself in all his grotesqueness and shrieking the most awful of sounds. Panic and terror ensued causing the poor victims to flee for their lives.

But this was put to good use apparently during the Battle of Marathon when Athens was defending itself against the attacking Persians. Pan had met the messenger sent to Sparta for assistance, and asked him why the Athenians didn't worship him. *"Tell them"* said Pan, *"I'll help them in their hour of need if they agree to pay me some respect."* The aid Pan gave was to show the Athenian warriors how to startle the life out of their adversaries, and they charged upon them with great speed and much noise, covering huge distances at a time. So filled with dread were the Persians at the ferocity of the Greek advance that they fled in terror and Athens won the day. In tribute a sanctuary was established in a cave beneath the Acropolis, from which the worship of Pan spread throughout Greece.

One of the most lasting legacies of Pan is the 'you either hate them or love them' panpipes, made famous more recently by South American musicians. Among Pan's delights was to chase and 'enjoy' the wood nymphs of Arcadia. One day he was pursuing Syrinx, a particularly beautiful creature who kept company with Artemis, the virgin goddess. As Pan was about to grab her,

Illustration from ancient sculpture, old 'Blackies' school book

she cried out for help to the river gods, who immediately turned her into a bed of reeds. Distraught at losing his conquest, Pan took up a bunch of the reeds and was entranced by the sweet music they made as the wind blew across them. He promptly took seven of different lengths and bound them together. He called the resulting instrument his Syrinx in memory of his lost love, but we know it better as the panpipes.

His musical prowess developed to the extent that one day he challenged Apollo, claiming he could make a sweeter melody than the master of the lyre. Only his friend King Midas, however,

was prepared to vote against the senior of the gods, for which in punishment Apollo gave him the ears of an ass.

Funny fellow, wicked womaniser, dreadful monster frightening people to death, but for all that, protector of all those who loved and worked with nature. Was he a mere invention of the primitive mind of man, or is he still alive and well in the thoughts and minds of all those of us who have ever been scared or had a bad day, or even just needed an excuse to go a little mad? Maybe there's a little bit of *Pan* in *ALL* of us!

Ancient Greek Chaos Theory *by Terry Cook*

So how did it all begin? According to the Ancient Greeks, first there was **Chaos** (a vast and dark space without shape or light) and then **Gaea** (mother or 'deep-breasted' earth) appeared out of Chaos, forming the place where men and gods would one day live. Next **Tartarus**, the swirling mists where rebellious ones would be imprisoned, and **Eros**, the handsome and passion-making deity who stops the senses and reasoning of gods and men alike, to give the vital key to bearing life. Then lastly from the chasm that was the beginning of all things sprang **Erebus**, the darkness of the underworld beneath Gaea, and **Nyx**, the night above her.

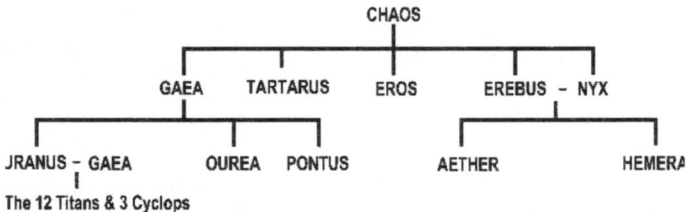

The 12 Titans & 3 Cyclops

So with Eros present to work the magic, Erebus and Nyx made love and Nyx gave birth to **Aether**, the upper sky with the bluest azure cloak stretched far above the earth, then his sister, **Hemera**, the day, was born. Stepping out of the mists of Tartarus, she brought brilliant light, returning to her mother as twilight fell, to sleep and rest until beckoned to rise again, and again...

Now Gaea, touched with Eros' power, brought forth herself a lover, **Uranus**, the heavens, clothed in dark silk embroidered with glittering stars, which would be the home of all the gods. Not finished yet, Gaea writhed again to bear **Ourea** (the mountains) and **Pontus** (the seas that would never drain).

With the universe in place, Gaea's passions turned on Uranus and from the union of heaven and earth, the **Titans** were born. They were the first race and brought to creation the personalities and eccentrics which have since developed into what we know as **The Olympian Gods** and **Mankind**.

Greek Language

Vocabulary - House Buying & Building *by Terry Cook*

Learning Greek is easiest at classes or from course books, but if you only learn 'holiday' Greek and decide to realise your dream of living in Greece, you may find that buying property or building and renovating terms and words are not included in standard lessons. If you can construct some simple sentences and communicate with Greek people, the following vocabulary could come in very useful. Be aware that there are often colloquial regional alternatives.

For buying or finalising house purchase/building:

το συμβόλαιο	=	contract
η αγορά	=	purchase (also used for market)
ο συμβολαιογράφος	=	notary
ο δικηγόρος	=	lawyer (for conveyancing)
η άδεια οικοδομής	=	building licence
ο εργολάβος οικοδομών	=	building contractor
ο πολιτικός μηχανικός	=	civil engineer
το τοπογραφικό (σκαρίφημα)	=	rough/outline plan
το σχέδιο	=	building plan (design)
η πολεοδομία	=	town planning (office)
η νομαρχία	=	prefecture (like County Council)
η ακίνητη περιουσία	=	real estate, immovable property
το οικόπεδο	=	building plot

Tradesmen:

ο κτίστης	=	builder
ο τουβλάς	=	bricklayer
ο μαραγκός	=	carpenter
ο μπογιατζής	=	[house] painter
ο ηλεκτρολόγος	=	electrician
ο υδραυλικός	=	plumber
ο σοβατζής	=	plasterer
ο μάστορας	=	expert, master craftsman
ο εργάτης	=	labourer

Structural & Building Work:

τα χαλάσματα	=	demolitions
το πέταμα μπάζων	=	removal of rubbish
κτίζω	=	to build
τα θεμέλια	=	foundations

η πισίνα	=	swimming pool
η σκεπή (ενός σπιτιού) / η στέγη	=	roof (of a house)
μια σκεπή με κεραμίδια	=	a tiled roof
μια σκεπή με ταράτσα	=	a flat roof (with terrace)
η πλάκα τσιμέντου	=	concrete slab (for flat roof)
το μπετόν	=	concrete
το μπετόν αρμέ	=	reinforced concrete
τα τούβλα	=	bricks
τα δοκάμια	=	rafters
ο σοβάς	=	plaster
η μόνωση	=	insulation
το ρεύμα	=	electricity
η σύνδεση	=	connection
η τηλεφωνική σύνδεση	=	telephone connection
τα υδραυλικά	=	plumbing
η αποχέτευση	=	drains, drainage, sewerage
η ξυλουργική	=	carpentry
τα καθαρίσματα	=	cleaning

Fixtures and Fittings:

το παράθυρο	=	window, casement
η κάσα (κουφωμάτων)	=	window-frame
το παραθυρόφυλλο	=	shutter
βάζω τζάμια	=	to glaze (put on glass panes)
το αλουμίνιο	=	aluminium
η ποδιά (παραθύρου)	=	window-sill
το κατώφλι	=	doorstep, threshold
τα σκαλοπάτια	=	stairs, steps
το πάτωμα	=	floor
ξύλινο πάτωμα	=	wooden floor
τα πλακάκια τοίχου / πατώματος	=	wall tiles / floor tiles
το λούκι	=	gutter, drainpipe
το χρώμα / η μπογιά	=	paint
ο διακόπτης	=	switch
ο γενικός διακόπτης	=	mains switch
η πρίζα	=	power-socket
η φίσα	=	plug

το φως	=	light
η λάμπα	=	lamp, bulb
το καλώδιο	=	cable, wire
το κουτί (ο πίνακας)	=	fuse-box
η ασφάλεια	=	fuse
η σωλήνα	=	pipe, tube, conduit
οι σωλήνες νερού	=	water-pipes
το καρφί	=	nail
η βίδα	=	screw

Crossword for Students of Greek by Margy Gulland

Σταυρόλεξο

Try to complete the crossword with the Greek answers, without using a dictionary first.

(Answers on page 187)

Οριζόντιος
1. **shop**
5. **vocabulary**
7. **frame**
8. **why**
9. **capable** (neuter)
11. **aimless** (feminine)
12. **article** (neuter sing.)
13. **resurrection** (genitive)

Κατακόρυφος
1. **fine weather**
2. **journeys**
3. **club / society**
4. **receipt**
6. **full** (accusative plur.)
10. **church**
12. **article** (neuter plur.)

Language Difficulties

This confusing sign from *Linda Terrill* was spotted at the entrance to Kalifteri Beach, Afissos, Pelion - so presumably it is OK to Trespass?

ΔΙΩΤΙΚΟΣ ΧΩΡΟΣ
ΔΙΕΛΕΥΣΗ ΜΟΝΟ
ΓΙΑ ΠΑΡΑΛΙΑ

PRIVATE PROPERTY
TRESPASSING TO THE
BEACH ONLY

... from *Derek Robson*, this rather macabre sign was seen at an idyllic spot on Lefkas *"I was told the 'death freezer' is the body-storage facility (Mortuary). We only found a small brick building with no sign (nor smell) but we did not find the lake."*

... and from **Paul Burlison** an interesting English translation error in a Hania 'Panorama' booklet *"The prefecture of Hania has reached a tourist orgasm"* !

The Itch... *by Jackie Bott*

"I've got an itch" said my husband one evening, emerging almost wet from his dribble of a shower. A mosquito had got him? A flea off one of the resident dogs - or something else? Careful inspection revealed a little train of small red blisters beneath a crease of flesh on his chest. That looks familiar, thought I: sweat rash - my prickly heat cream should clear it up in no time, and accordingly liberally applied it to him, assuming all would be well soon.

The next day dawned. No change, so I gave the rash another dose of cream, but my beloved was still scratching rather a lot. *"Town for breakfast?"* he said, *"why not - an hour's leg stretch down the road will do us good."* Omelettes, coffee, freshly squeezed orange juice and flick-the-flies-off-the-bread, while watching the world go by in the harbour. Intoxicated by the smell of mopeds, ferries and hydrofoils, pleasantly replete but with the itching getting worse, we headed for my favourite shop - the Pharmacy - so many of my ills having been cured there during previous visits.

No-one else was in the shop, and peering round in the semi-light, we were spotted and the lights sprang to life. Ever vigilant and attentive, the Pharmacist asked if we needed any help. In our experience the quickest and easiest way of obtaining a diagnosis for a problem was to simply indicate it, or act out the symptoms, so my love lifted up his T-shirt and pointed to the offending rash. *"Is it a heat rash?"* we enquired. *"Does it hurt?"* asked the Pharmacist. *"No, it just itches."* *"Aaaahhh"* he pronounced, paused, and added *"Herpes."* *"Herpes?"* we asked, aghast. *"Ne, herpes"* he replied *"go Health Centre, see Doctor."* *"Efaristo, we'll do that."*

We left the shop and had a brief and dumbfounded discussion outside - how on earth had hubby contracted a sexually transmitted disease when we'd been married for 15 years? And being as we'd been on the island for three days, had he given it to me while we'd been sharing bath towels, a bed, and the water bottle?

Setting off for the Health Centre, we were stopped in our tracks by the Pharmacist calling us *"come back, Doctor is here"*. Retracing our steps into the gloomy interior, the T-shirt was again lifted, an inspection made, and the pronouncement given *"Herpes! – antibiotics"*. The tablets cost us £60 and were to be taken twice a day for seven days, with no more than one glass of wine permitted a day, and he must stay out of the sun. A wonderful prospect for two week's holiday for a sun-worshipper, *and* with a 40th birthday party on the horizon.

So shamed were we at the thought of Herpes that we daren't mention it to anyone. Several people commented on my dear one being quiet, and not having a drink, *"throat infection, poor love"* we lied, and much sympathy followed. We finally cracked and mentioned the dreaded lurgy to some close Greek friends. *"Oh yes"*, said one, *"had that myself, and so did Elios."* *"I had it for years, and it kept recurring"* said another. We wondered just how promiscuous they were, as we discarded the beaker we'd both been drinking from, along with a few other communal bits, and took to kissing on the cheek only.

My husband spent a week swinging in a shaded hammock by the pool, and sleeping a lot, while we kept our dirty secret to ourselves. He dutifully took the tablets and the rash went down.

On returning to England we went straight to see our own Doctor, an emergency appointment on a Saturday morning in the days when you could actually see a Doctor on a weekend. *"Oh yes"* he said *"Shingles."* *"Shingles?"* we enquired *"we were told in Greece that it's Herpes - you know, that rather dodgy disease."* *"Oh no"* he replied *"same virus, different strain, don't worry."* Well, we had, hadn't we, and needlessly too!

We still laugh about it today, whenever one of us has an itch or a rash, and forgave our dear Greek friends for not being promiscuous after all.

Greek Howlers

from E R Jenkinson

What a difference one letter can make! After a couple of years of adult education 'Holiday Greek' lessons I'd managed to use a few everyday expressions without calamities - until one evening we were eating in a taverna in Katelios, Kefalonia. Unusually there was no cruet on the table, so I asked the waiter "Μπορούμε να εχουμε λάδι και φίδι." wanting the oil & vinegar (ξίδι). He looked at me and howled with laughter - then explained that I'd asked for oil and a *snake*! The English people sitting nearby didn't understand, so I didn't feel too bad. Yiannis appreciated my attempts to speak Greek, so we became good friends for the rest of our stay.

Back home and at my classes again, I had a piece of homework on 'Do you like - Does it please you' returned with the words *"Check your dictionary!"* from my tutor. I had written "Σου αρέσει η καινούργια μου τσόντα;" Of course I should have written 'τσάντα' for 'Do you like my new handbag?'. In the dictionary for 'τσόντα' it says 'inset, gusset, or porno flash!'. She does still speak to me.

from Colin Hunter

About 8 years ago my wife and I and our girls went to Lesvos, staying in Petra. Whilst walking through the village, I decided we needed milk. I had just started Greek lessons at night school and could not wait to try communicating with the natives. Into the supermarket I went, my wife waited outside. It was a decent sized shop and after a lot of rummaging I could find no fresh milk. Here goes, I thought. Taking a deep breath I went to the Greek man at the till and in my best Greek asked if he had any fresh milk. I stood there very proud of myself.

He looked at me and said in English *"I am sorry sir, we are still waiting for the sheep."* 30 seconds later I was still standing looking at the man very confused wondering what to say. *"I thought it came from cows"* I said. It was his turn to look confused now.

I stepped out of the door and my wife said *"What's wrong? You look puzzled."* I told her what happened. She said *"I think he meant the 'ship' - with supplies from the mainland."*

It took me quite a while to stop laughing.

Book Reviews

Reviews by *Sylvia Cook* (except where indicated)

Eurydice Street by Sofka Zinovieff

Publisher: Granta Book ISBN 186207-681-2 £14.99

Not only a personal account of life in Athens with her Greek husband returning to his roots and their two children learning to become Greek. With her journalist's eye and anthropologist's interest in people, Sofka explores modern Greek life. She talks to friends and relatives to understand the background that has shaped today's Athenians. I often found myself referring to Sofka's comments in conversation. 'Athens Street Dogs' in Greek-o-File Volume 2 was a taster adapted from this book.

The House of the Eagle by Duncan Sprott

Publisher: Faber & Faber ISBN 0571 20285 3 £12.99

From humble beginnings as a Macedonian soldier, the first Ptolemy becomes king then pharaoh of Egypt after Alexander's death. The Ptolomies Quartet chronicles his dynasty which survived 300 years in spite of unending wars, intrigues, family alliances, incestuous marriages and disasters around the Greek world. Narrated by *Thoth*, the Egyptian God of writing and wisdom, the style is a little strange at times, but brings to life a colourful family and a period in history when Egypt and the Greek world were one. Volumes 2 is due March 2005.

The Moon Maiden by S V Peddle

Publisher: Blackie & Co ISBN 184470-018-6 £6.99

This first novel of a 'bull-dancers' trilogy set in ancient Minoan Crete follows the fortunes and fate of Thasos, a young boy exiled with his family and cast out to sea. They are rescued and taken by the 'Keftiu' who introduce them to a different world of rituals, the Bull Court and the Moon Goddess. As Thasos grows up he feels more at ease outside the Knossos temple and is befriended by the huntress and goddess Britomartis of the old religion, but he is drawn back to the Bull Court, the Moon Maiden and his destiny. (See www.bulldancers.co.uk for more details & subsequent books.)

North of Ithaka by Eleni Gage

Publisher: Bantam ISBN 0593 05189 0 £16.99

Journalist daughter of Nicholas Gage, who wrote the acclaimed 'Eleni' about his mother's struggles, torture and murder during the Greek Civil War, Eleni Gage returns to Lia in the Epirot mountains to re-build her grandparent's home. She tells the inti-mate story of her 'journey home' to her paternal roots. Becoming a part of local village life as she oversees building work and gets to know the area, she reflects on her family's past and the traditions that are still so much a part of everyday life. At

times touching but also amusing and uplifting, Eleni succeeds in combining travel anecdotes and folklore discoveries with her personal memoirs.

Little Infamies by Panos Karnezis

Publisher: Jonathan Cape ISBN 0224-06261-1 £10

Written in English by a young Greek writer, this col-lection of short stories about the fictional people in an unnamed Greek village tells of their good, and mostly bad deeds. The stories intersect, so by the end you feel you know the villagers and their relationships. Some of the events related seem a little strange, some harsh and cruel, often amusing, but behind the sto-ries you sense a real world, created, observed and forgiven for its 'little infamies'.

Cassandra's Disk by Angela Green

Publisher: Peter Owen ISBN 07206-1144-X £10.95

Photographer Cassandra Byrd writes her memoirs from a sanctuary on Ithaka where she is dying. She races to recall everything, the sad, the bad, the rau-cous, the emotions, but mostly her relationship with her twin sister, now a successful and beautiful ac-tress. She sees herself as the 'big bad' sister, loved by her wonderful classics teacher father, who died when they were young, and hated by her mother. The Greek connection was the reason I got this book, but I was engrossed in the personalities and the duel between the two sisters and fascinated as the events and emotions of their lives unfolded.

Greek Salad by Miles Lambert-Gocs

Publisher: Ambeli Press & Wine Appreciation Guild
ISBN 1-891267-82-5 £9.95

Subtitled 'A Dionysian Travelogue', Miles writes of his odysseys around the islands and mainland Greece researching Greek wines for his previous book, The Wines of Greece, and wine articles for The Athenian Monthly. He tells the tales of characters he meets and incidents along the way, with background information on regions, traditions and of course the local food and wine that are his passion. An adaptation of one chapter is featured in this volume - A Diamond (Wine) in the Rough.

It's All Greek To Me by John Mole

Publisher: Nicholas Brealey ISBN 1-85788-343-8 £9.99

John Mole bought a view (from a dilapidated house) outside an Evvian village 25 years ago. At the time he was working in Athens with his wife and 4 young children and reluctant to return to Britain. His family were appalled at his rashness, although when his wife saw the view she too could imagine their own 'Arcadia'. The children were also pleased believing they were to get an amusement arcade! As he rebuilds the house in the old style and gets to grips with the local people, they in turn get used to him - particularly his often amusing Greek language attempts. A witty fun-filled book which recreates a rustic Greece now rarely found.

Greece on My Wheels by Edward Enfield

Publisher: Somersdale ISBN 184024 2809 £7.99 - review by Georges Jurish

Thought I'd share a little jewel with you and all the other 'Greek-o-philes'. Amongst the things I had for my birthday back in August was a book written by Edward Enfield (Harry's dad) entitled 'Greece on my Wheels'. I saved it to take to Crete on holiday and read it almost without putting it down.

It tells about two cycling trips he made (hence the title). The first part of the book concerns a circuit of the Peloponnese, and the second part is about another trip from Corfu down to Mesolongi. His writing style is brilliant, very dry and humorous, and I can recommend it as a thoroughly good read - particularly on holiday and especially for those who appreciate the Greek culture.

Southern Peloponnese by Michael Cullen

Publisher: Sunflower ISBN 1-85691-224-8 £11

These handy 10x21cm 136-pages walking and tour-ing guides are well presented and packed with both driving and walking tour suggestions, with area and local maps and colour photographs to bring the routes alive. The Southern Peloponnese guide had 5 car tours and 30 walks to choose from or com-bine to find a surprising variety of hidden 'authentic Greece' areas. Having a limited time to explore, we used the driving tour description for The Mani to decide where to stop and explore. Although we chose to go in the opposite direction (a good choice as it turns out) the descriptions, background infor-mation, opening times, facilities and detour descrip-tions were just as useful. The walks for the area seemed well described, with helpful timings, for independent walkers to find the most interesting and scenic routes.

Other Greek Sunflower Landscapes include Corfu, Eastern Crete, Western Crete, Samos, Lesvos and due 2005 Paxos & Kefalonia.

Guide to Biblical Sites in Greece & Turkey by Clyde Fant & Mitchell Reddish

Publisher: Oxford University Press
ISBN 019-513918-6 £15.99

The rear cover synopsis "Easy to use and abundantly illustrated, this unique book will help visitors to appre-ciate the rich history, significance and wonder of the ancient world of the Bible" describes this book well. With its clear and concise layout, you don't have to be reli-gious to enjoy the living history conjured up by the two scholars responsible for this work.

Heavens Above by Alan Carter

Publisher: Efstathiadis ISBN 960-226-603-1 £5.99 from Gazelle (p184). Subtitled 'The Greek Connection'.

Alan Carter describes the universe - planets, satellites, stars and constellations in a simple informative way - then the stories of the relevant Greek gods, goddesses and myths. The Greek legends are often more believ-able than the astronomical scale of the facts.

Flavours of Greece by Rosemary Barron

Publisher: Grub Street ISBN 1 904010 61 X £12.99

Now published in paperback, this collection of over 250 regional and national specialities and notes on Greek foods, kitchen tools and wines is presented in a way that always appeals to me. Although there are few colour pictures, Rosemary's introductory paragraphs for each recipe offer background information, personal anecdotes, advice on ingredients or accompaniments. The more complicated methods are simply explained (as in Chicken with Avgolemono sauce p.135) and simple dishes are not spoilt by unnecessary flourishes. Rosemary is clearly a Grecophile as well as an accomplished cook and cookery writer.

The Real Cost of Building a House in Greece by R & E Rhodes

Direct from authors £15 inc UK P&P. (p185)

This well presented 100 page A4 book includes a CD with photo gallery and linked Excel spreadsheets to help you estimate the cost of building your dream home on a plot of land in Greece. Based on Elaine & Dusty Rhodes' personal experiences and local experts in NW Crete where they built their brick house with pool, there is a lot of good advice, including project management and letting considerations. The spreadsheets may need amendment in places to vary costs for your circumstances, but will certainly make you think before you act.

The Ancient Greek Computer from Rhodes by Victor J. Kean

Publisher: Efstathiadis ISBN 960 226 227 3 £2.99 from Gazelle (p184)

It's true - the ancient Greeks had computers. Well, at least one. This little 90 page booklet tells the story of the Antikythera Mechanism. Part 1 explores the 'possible' history of an amazing device invented in the 1st century BC in Rhodes to plot the movement of stars and planets and thus predict the future. Part 2 explains how it was recovered from a shipwreck off Antikythera in 1910 and has baffled the world of science for nearly 100 years. Now in Athens Museum it has generated a fascinating tale, well told. *(Terry Cook)*

Journey to the Holy Mountain: by Christopher Merrill

Publisher: Harper Collins ISBN 0 0 711901 1 £17.99

Subtitled 'Meditations on Mount Athos'. We passed it to John Arnell (ref article in Greek Life) for his comments.

The Holy Mountain seen from the perspective of a poet and journalist recently returned from reporting on the war in Bosnia. This is a spiritual autobiography as well as a guide to the monasteries, their history and the lives of the monks living there today, based on three recent visits by the author. He also reflects on the impact of these visits on his own life and understanding. It is well written, a thoroughly engrossing read and a good introduction to Mount Athos. I recommend it. *(John Arnell)*

Exploring the Greek Mosaic by Benjamin J Broome

Publisher: Intercultural Press Inc, ISBN 1-877864-39-0 £12.99

The sub title of this book is 'A Guide to Intercultural Communication in Greece' which is what it is. Although presented as a study work to aid American managers, diplomats and students who need to interact with Greeks, anyone who loves Greece will appreciate the flowing style of text, analysing (as far as they can be analysed) the Greek ways and searching for cultural patterns. It could provide a useful insight to Greek life, family, religion, conversation and conflict in relationships for anyone intending to make their home in Greece.

Syntax of the Modern Greek Verbal System by Rolf Hesse

Publisher: Museum Tusculanum Press Denmark ISBN 87 7289 823 2 £23 - available from Gazelle (p184)

The title says what it is and although many readers would not want to know more, serious students of Greek would find this book useful to improve their understanding of the way Greek verbs are used today. More a study work than a reference book, giving numerous examples from literary authors and current linguistic practice. A 'celebration' of the great reforms in the Greek language which have been achieved since its simplification in the 1970s. *(Terry Cook)*

Events

UK Hellenic Clubs & Societies

There are a number of official societies and 'friendship' clubs set up throughout the UK to bring together British and Greek people to share their interest in Greece. Below are those we were able to track down and check. Meeting town, contact details and events are given below in North to South sequence, London last. Do contact those near you for venue, event and membership details and let us know of any more for our records.

Aberdeen Scottish Hellenic Society
Verna Ward, 012 2458 7476, verna@singing.f9.co.uk
Monthly on university campus - lectures & parties.

St Andrews - Scottish Hellenic Society
Tom Harrison, tehh@st-and.ac.uk, www.st-andrews.ac.uk/~greeks
Monthly at St Andrews Univ - academic talks, films & social evenings.

Manchester - Hellenic Brotherhood
Mr Andreas Yiasoumi, 0161 962 1342
Saturday School at Salford Orthodox church - for children to learn Greek.

Birmingham - The Greek Club
John & Doreen Fryer, 012 1523 7223, thefryers@dial.pipex.com
Monthly 1st Thurs. at Birmingham Univ - social evenings, talks mainly on history & culture.

Worcester - The Kefi Club
Nick Kontarines - 01684 566323, kontarines@btinternet.com
Monthly last Fri. - talks & social evenings.

Worcester Anglo-Hellenic Friendship Club
David Leggott, 019 0521 1886
Monthly last Thurs. at Maple Leaf pub - talks, holiday ideas & social evenings.

Hillingdon Anglo Greek Club
Lena Markou, 01895 631 865, lena_markou@hotmail.com
     or P. Klimis 020 8868 6746
Monthly 1st Fri. at Ickenham Adult Ed. Centre - talks & social evenings.

Egham, Surrey - Friends of the Hellenic Institute
Jonathan Harris, 01784 443086/443311, Jonathan.Harris@rhul.ac.uk
Royal Holloway College, www.rhul.ac.uk/hellenic-institute.

Portsmouth Anglo-Hellenic Society
Demetris Papanicolaou, 023 9286 3566
Monthly 3rd Fri. Southsea Community Assn - social evenings & talks.
Language & dance meetings other days.

LONDON - THE HELLENIC CENTRE
Evangelia Roussos, 020 7487 5060, www.helleniccentre.org
At The Hellenic Centre, 16-18 Paddington Street, London W1U 5AS
Talks, lectures, music, art, films, social events & library.

Societies meeting at Hellenic Centre (c/o Hellenic Centre if not specified)

Book Club
Monthly discussion meetings in Hellenic Centre Library

Cretan Association of Great Britain
Emmanuel Stavrianakis, 020 8445 4401, stavrianakis@hotmail.com
Occasional lectures & functions, annual dinner plus exhibitions.

Greek Archaeological Committee UK
Lectures

Ionian Society

London Hellenic Society
Lectures on various subjects

Macedonian Society of Great Britain
sec@macedonian.org.uk,www.macedonia.org.uk

London W11 - Foundation for Hellenic Culture
020 7499 9826, www.greece.inbritain.org.uk
UK wide Greece in Britain Events organised.

London WC1 - Society for the Promotion of Hellenic Studies
020 7862 8730 / Library 020 7387 7697, hellenic@sas.ac.uk,
www.sas.ac.uk/icls/hellenic
Academic lectures, library.

London WC2 - Dept of Byzantine & Modern Greek Studies, Kings College
Dr. Karabod, 020 7873 2088
Academic lectures & seminars at Kings College.

London SW10 - Anglo-Hellenic League
Suzanne Drummond, 020 7486 9410, anglohellenic.league@virgin.net
Publish a review twice a year, Annual Runciman award ceremony

London & Harrow, Middx - Peloponnesian Association of Great Britain
020 8732 2833, PeloponnesiansGB@aol.com
Meets various places for dances, talks (some English, some Greek) & informal
meetings, all related to the Peloponnese - open to members & visitors.

European Football Champions *by Graeme Dakin*

100 to 1 outsiders! Having never won a game in the final stages of an international tournament, this appeared to sum up the Greek team's chances. However, Greece had arrived at the European Championships by topping their qualifying group as part of a 15 match unbeaten run. The traditionally skilful (but very individual) Greek players had been moulded into a hard-working, resilient team by their German coach, Otto Rehhagel, and were determined to do their country proud.

Greece stormed through their qualifying group by beating the hosts Portugal and the highly regarded Spanish team. Ahead lay the defending champions France, who many experts expected to retain their title. The Greek team showed scant respect for the reputation of the French team and battled gallantly to cause the upset of the tournament by beating them 1-0. The Czech Republic, new favourites for the championship, were to be Greece's opponents in the semifinals.

I arrived in Crete shortly before this semifinal and although there was an undercurrent of interest and hope, it appeared that most Greeks were in a mild state of shock. Flags were evident, occasionally on vehicles, but on nothing like the scale that the flag of St. George was seen in England. The semifinal attracted a fair but not great number of spectators in the tavernas and bars of Plaka and Almiridha (east of Chania), but there were more groans than cheers as the Greeks battled to subdue the more fancied Czechs. The tension mounted as the match moved into extra time. At the final touch of the first half, a headed 'silver' goal by Dellas won the game for Greece.

The tension lifted and a huge roar echoed around the bay. Then fireworks exploded, rifles were shot into the air and convoys of cars started touring the villages with their horns blaring loudly. This continued deep into the night with the realisation that they were now in the final and just one game away from the seemingly impossible. Ships in Souda Bay blasted their foghorns and a priest in the quiet hill village of Gavolochori was so moved by the result that he rang the church bells at midnight. Football fever gripped the country as never before. The Greek flag appeared everywhere and pictures of the team were displayed in many shop windows.

Preparations were made for the final on Sunday 4th July and huge parties were planned regardless of the result. Locals and tourists packed the tavernas and bars on another oppressive night to watch. Again, the Greeks were very much on the defensive as the Portuguese, roared on by their home crowd, surged forward in wave after wave of attacks. The outstanding Greek teamwork and safe hands of their goalkeeper, Nikopolidis, kept the score goalless at half-time. The tension was etched on the faces of the watching

Greek youths as the match followed the same pattern in the early part of the second-half - and then the impossible. A corner from the right was headed in by the Greek striker Charisteas and Greece led 1-0 in the 57th minute! The bar erupted and there was riotous singing and dancing

Many fans made it to Lisbon - pictured here at Athens airport midday 4th July by Sylvia Cook

with the repeated chant of *"Hellas! Hellas! Hellas!"*.

Fingers were chewed to the knuckles and brows became more deeply furrowed as Greece was subjected to intense Portuguese pressure, but the team defended courageously with the goalkeeper excelling. As the match entered the final minute of normal time, the fourth official indicated that 5 minutes of injury time would be played. Whistles of disapproval showed everyone's feelings towards this additional period of torture. Time appeared to stand still, but then the referee blew the final whistle. There was a momentary silence before the bar went wild at the realisation that their impossible dream had come true.

Again, *"Hellas ! Hellas ! Hellas !"* chants rang out as the whole bar went mad. Champagne was sprayed, drinks were knocked back in triumph and to ease throats dry from the extreme tension, *"Zagorakis! Zagorakis! Zagorakis!"* was sung in tribute to the much revered Greek captain (named Man of the Match and later Player of the Tournament). People were jumping and dancing around while a few just sat with their heads in their hands trying to take in what had happened. The diminutive barmaid, complete with a Greek Flag 'cape', was hoisted onto the shoulders of one of the dancing youths from where she directed the singing enthusiastically. Throughout the area, partying started in earnest. Fireworks, guns and horn blaring cars noisily celebrated the win. A convoy led by a mobile crane lorry started a circuit between Almiridha and Plaka with horns blaring, continuing until the early hours of morning.

Greece had done it against all the odds and what a pleasure it was to see such a proud nation celebrate the victorious achievement of their team in a game they love but had previously struggled at in international competition.

Legacy of the Athens Olympics *by Sylvia & Terry Cook*

"Will it be ready?" was the question on everyone's lips before the August 2004 28th Olympiad in Athens. IT WAS! Out of chaos emerged a well organised event that will leave a lasting legacy. Like middle distance runner Kelly Holmes, the UK's double gold-medallist, Athens seemed to hold back till the last minute, then sprint home to a fantastic finish.

A resounding success that will not only be remembered for the 'Greekness' of the spectacular opening and closing ceremonies depicting Greece from the ancient Olympic games through to a modern Greece that seductively

AΘHNA 2004

combines its eastern and western influences; the emotions of athletes winning, trying, or just pleased to take part; the triumph of successful athletes who worked hard for their supremacy over cheating drug users who were clearly made unwelcome; the trouble free security and safety in difficult times; and the 'state of the art' modern stadia that enabled spectators in Athens and many millions more around the world to witness this celebration of sport and sportsmanship at its best.

Just as the site of the ancient Olympics at Olympia, last used in the 4th century AD, was the emotive setting for the 2004 Shot put without the intrusion of modern paraphernalia, and the Panathinaikos Stadium from the first modern Olympics of 1896 was the venue for the Archery, so the new Olympic facilities will be available for many years to come. New and renovated Sports Centres have won international acclaim - the Athens Olympic Sports Complex with the main stadium for Athletics, the Tennis Centre, the Indoor Hall for Gymnastics and Basketball, the Aquatic Centre and the Velodrome for cycling. The old Hellinikon Airport site was transformed into a sports complex for Baseball, Softball, a Canoe Kayak Slalom Centre and two indoor halls for a variety of other sports. Near historic Marathon on the coast the Schinias Rowing and Canoeing centre and various other locations now offer excellent facilities in breathtaking surroundings.

The transport system which effortlessly moved athletes, spectators and 'the media' around these sites and to their hotels and rooms, was put in place over the last 7 years for these Olympic games - but has given Athens a much needed lift to now surpass the facilities of many other modern capital cities. The new Elefterios Venizelos Airport, the new Suburban railway linking Athens' Larissis Station to the airport, extensions to the Metro, including

one to the airport, and the new Tram Light Railway linking Athens to the coastal resorts and Olympic facilities on the Saronic Gulf.

One of the most spectacular sights must be the Rio-Antirio bridge - 2,250 metres of graceful cable suspension engineering achievement. Linking the north and south banks of the Corinth Gulf, and the longest bridge of its kind in the world, it was opened in time for the Olympic Flame Relay to cross en route to Athens.

Much of the millions spent, was surely due to be spent on these improvements anyway. The Olympic timing was the fillip needed to bring about a speedy modernisation of Athens' transport infrastructure.

Let us hope too that Greece will benefit from the lessons learned by greedy businesses who raised their prices beyond acceptable levels in the hope of milking sports enthusiasts and visitors from around the world. Many found they still had unbooked rooms or flights as the Olympic date loomed, forcing them to reduce rates at the last minute. This had a catastrophic effect on the tourism industry throughout Greece where early expectations of increased visitors to Greece lead to higher prices demanded from the tour operators who set their brochure prices more than a year in advance. The result, less tourists to Greek resorts in the Olympic year and many tour operators struggling to fill prebooked flights and hotels as casual holidaymakers elected to spend their resources where they could get more for their money. Even some regular visitors decided to give Greece a miss in 2004.

The sales target of 3.4 million Olympic Games tickets was surpassed (3,581,080 tickets were sold), although there may have been some untaken seats. More athletes competed than before, 11,099 athletes from 202 countries, and more volunteers came forward to help at this Games. All a remarkable achievement for one of the smaller countries in the world.

Hopefully the television coverage, newspaper and magazine articles devoted not only to the games, but to the background of the Olympics and Greece will have encouraged many who have not yet visited Greece that it is a 'must see' country. The enthusiasm of Gianna Angelopoulos-Daskalaki, president of the organising committee for the Athens games, the Greek volunteers, the background scenery to outdoor events, the opening pageant, the traditional dancing and singing at the closing ceremony often brought a tear to our eyes and made us proud to be associated with Greece - albeit as outsiders.

So, in the words of the IOC president Jacques Rogge in his closing speech "Ευχαριστούμε Αθήνα, ευχαριστούμε Ελλάδα" Thank you Athens, thank you Greece - it was a wonderful experience, 'a dream games', and long may the legacy of the 2004 Athens Olympics live on.

Music

A Mix of Greek Rhythms *by Tony Davis*

When Tony Davis, a music and piano teacher by profession, volunteered to write about Greek Rhythms for us, I was intrigued as to how this could be explained in writing, but hopefully by following his practice lessons you will soon appreciate some of the typically Greek, but unusual, musical rhythms.

If you stay in Greece for a couple of weeks in a popular resort you could hear 'Zorba's Dance' many times over, with at least one demonstration of the syrtaki dance. The twangy (originally Turkish) bouzouki at once says

"Greece!" while the constant *"PLONK plink PLONK plink"*, in context, says *"Zorba"*, but that PLONK plink 2-beat metre could underpin music from almost anywhere.

The 2-beat metre and the 3-beat *'DUM ta ta'* underlie much Greek music, including the Cretan, among the very best folk music on the planet. But listening to a fair amount of Greek music you could feel there's something odd about its rhythm - equally with much folk music from south east Europe and some west European music up to about 1700.

Well, here's your chance to take practical steps to get right inside some of the 'odd' Greek rhythms - metres, strictly speaking. Then you will be able to physically or mentally dance along with them in tavernas, or (just mentally) in the overflowing bus lurching round hairpin bends with rebetika music blaring.

First, a warm-up on familiar ground.

With the palm of your left hand and your right hand fingertips you can alternately tap at a steady pace on a (steady!) table, mimicking the *'LOW high LOW high'* 2-beat metre of the well known home-grown music of example 1.

It has the words of the song written above a string of quavers, which represent the 2-beat metre. The lower notes are for the left palm and the others

Example 1 - Vertical barlines divide music into bars

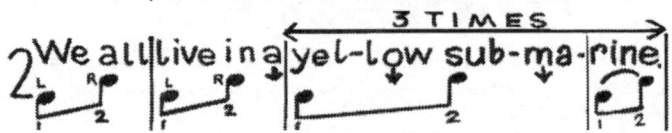

are for the right fingers. While you beat *'LOW high LOW high'* you speak the words in time with the beating. Mostly each syllable should coincide with the left or right beat under it, but the *'a'* comes <u>between</u> two beats (the arrow emphasises that) and the 'low' of 'yellow' and 'ma' of 'submarine' likewise. Slipping these notes in produces quick notes - BUT the hands continue at constant speed. The 'ine' of 'submarine' spreads across two notes - hence the slur (curved line).

In the simplest partnership of words and music the stronger syllables occur on the stronger notes, so the rhythm of the sung words is the same as with the spoken ones - eg *'sub-ma-<u>rine</u>',* not *'sub-<u>ma</u>-rine'.* Quite a lot of vocal music breaks that rule, but we need to keep to it for this exercise.

From now on we will use all the examples in the same way. Get familiar with ***'We** all **live** in a **yel**-low <u>sub</u>-ma-**<u>rine</u>'.* Take it slowly at first, you will get up to tear-away tempo sooner that way. When there is a hitch, restart from that point before your brain gets cluttered with something else and gradually lead into it from earlier and earlier in the piece as you gain greater control.

And so to example 2 which is more straightforward than *'Yellow submarine'*! That makes it easier to change it to a Greek rhythm later on.

Example 2

1. Choose an easy walking pace for your beats;
2. get the words ready;
3. notice the slurs (curved lines);
4. speak the words as indicated;
5. continue into the rest of the song (*'up above the world ....'*) in the same way.

Later try this variation:

Twin-kle, twinkle little star
3   L̂R   R   L̂R   R   L   R̂R   L̂RR etc

Now bring out the ouzo, retsina or Greek coffee because we now encounter the first of the mixed metres that still feature in much Greek music and give it an extra richness and variety.

Example 3

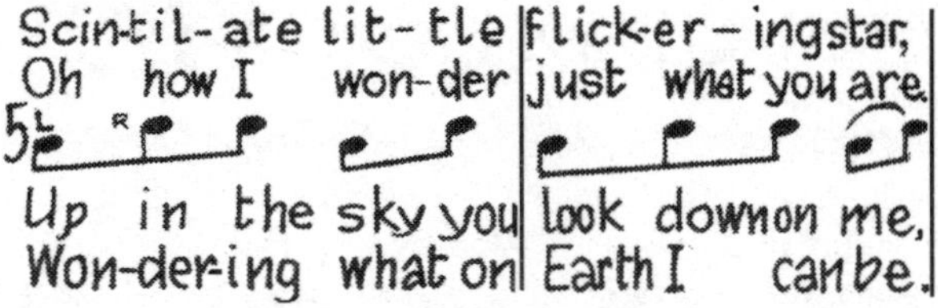

Scintil-ate lit-tle | flick-er-ingstar,
Oh how I won-der | just what you are.

Up in the sky you | look down on me,
Won-der-ing what on | Earth I can be.

Tackle this the same way as the previous examples. The unevenness of the main beats ('L' beats) might sound odd at first, but the 3 to 2 ratio (5-time) is a basic feature of most mixed metre music. A player picking out just these L beats must avoid simplifying the task by letting the ratio drift into 2 to 1. Have a go by beating the L beats on the table, but stabbing the air with the R forefinger so that only the L beat sounds : L (R R) L (R) etc. Notice the unevenness of the L beats though the beats (sounded and silent) are at a constant speed.

Example 4's metre is more common in Greek music than 5-time. We can frequently hear it in recordings of Islands music by (eg) Yiannis Parios and in music of the Greek population of old Smyrna (now Turkish Izmir) wonder-fully sung by Glykeria on her disc 'Smyrnika'.

Example 4

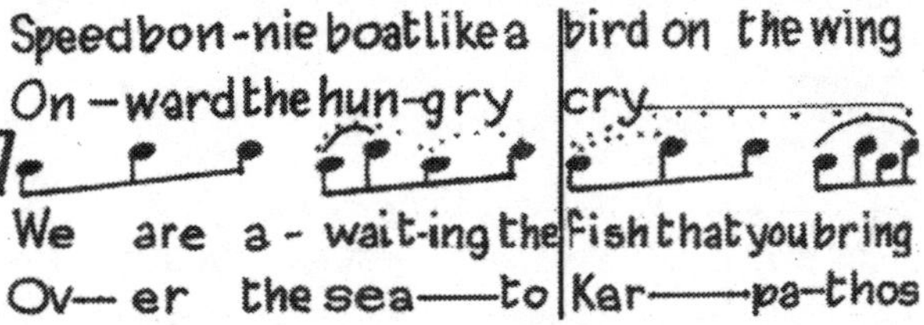

Speedbon-nieboatlikea | bird on the wing
On-wardthehun-gry | cry......

We are a-wait-ing the | fish thatyoubring
Ov-er the sea---to | Kar---pa-thos

Approach this example in the same way as the others. (Note that the island's name is <u>Kar</u>-pa-thos, not Kar-<u>pay</u>-thos, which would not fit the music anyhow.)

7-time music often has a lovely lilt, rather like the bobbing of a small boat on gentle waves. Here's a variation:-

Speed bon-nie boat like a | bird on the wing
7L R   R   L̂R L̂R   L RR   L̂RLR etc

Can you continue it?

Our next, example 5, is a frisky one, flipping between two metres as some in the rebetika style do. As with other examples, the words are chosen so as to produce a certain rhythm to fit the chosen metre. Some 4+5 pieces (or 5+4) are slow and dramatic, eg 'Τα δύο μάτια σας' (Your two eyes) which is included in a recording of rebetika pieces by N. Roussou.

Example 5   4-time = *LRLR* 5-time = *LRRLR* - *all beats at same speed*

	<u>1</u>	<u>2</u>	<u>3</u>	<u>4</u>	<u>5</u>
4	Oh **lit** - tle	**town** of	**My**-ko-nos __	Your	
5 :	**maze** of	**al** - leys	**led** the	**pi**- rates a-<u>stray</u>, which is	
4 :	**much** the	**same** as it	**is** to -	<u>day</u> with	
5 :	**hordes** of	sweat-y &	baf-fled	**tour** - ists	<u>lost</u> !

Singers and solo players often 'bend' the time (ie vary the speed) while the accompaniment keeps to the unvarying beat. It's the band you need to concentrate on if you want to focus on the metre.

The words of example 6 give the rhythm of a piece of laïka music (originally, roughly speaking, the Greek equivalent to western pop music, but closer to traditional music with features in common with rebetika). This one, 'Το κορίτσι μου ζιλέυει' (My girl is jealous), is still often heard on a recording made by its composer, B. Tzintani, over forty years ago. Its extra beat at the end of the bar tips you forward into the next bar.

Example 6

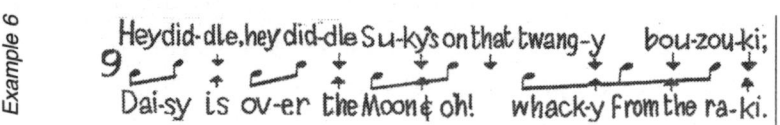

On a few occasions the whole band stamps out the metre :

	SLOW	SLOW	SLOW	QUICK	QUICK	QUICK
9	L (R)	L (R)	L (R)	L&R	L&R	L&R

Maybe you would like to try your hand at writing words for some more verses based on the nursery rhymes used so far.

(For a good explanation of rebetika and laïka see Chris William's article in The Greek-o-File Vol 1 p.173).

And now for a surprise ..... A Mozartian oddity: the opening of the minuet in Mozart's 40th Symphony.

By chance (surely!) much of this dark piece strides through a variety of Greek mixed metres. Though minuets are in normal 3-time, this one has many strong beats occurring in 'wrong' places, ie. it has syncopations, but Mozart wrote it supposedly in 3-time, with signs of where the syncopations (changes to beat) are. The piece continues in similar vein for about 8 times the length of our version (example 7), with a calm interlude before the final 3 times.

In our version the words give the rhythm of the melody and bar lines show where the strong beats occur, thus clearly showing the changing number of beats between them. This placing of bar lines is common practice in classical music since 1900, but was not in the 18th century, Mozart's time.

This medley of Greek mixed metres brings our table-thumping to a grand climax in an unexpected way, as befits a subject that, to 21st century Westerners, is an unusual twist in folk music.

Now you're on your own, (or maybe with someone), so you can start trying to hear these mixed metres in Greek music .... but how will you tell which metre a particular piece is in?

The chances are that it will be easy to identify 2-time (or 4-time in which one bar sounds very like 2 of 2-time, but no big deal which it is). 3-time is the other 'normal' time (LRR repeating). You need to identify the first beats of the bars (is it $\underline{1}$ 2, $\underline{1}$ 2, or $\underline{1}$ 2 3, $\underline{1}$ 2 3 ?) and table thump to the music as a strong physical test. If 2 or 3 don't work, then test for 7, especially if it is island music you are listening to. Rebetika and Laïka are good candidates for 9 and 4+5. 5-time is rather less likely in Greek music. Don't let 'bending' of time deceive you.

Please remember: don't make listening to Greek music become just an exercise in counting beats. (Some say beat-awareness is just maths, but maths is more than just counting!) The great thing is to try to catch the different **physical feel** of the varied metres and taste the different flavours.

Example 7

In Mozart's original, backing has strong notes after bar lines but not after (♩)

Now you can test yourself on these: (Answers page 187)

| = barline   ● = L   ⬻ = L or R (you decide)   ⌒ = 2 beats to 1 syllable

Remember - Syllables should be strong and weak as in normal speech: L beats stronger than R; notes <u>between</u> beats are weaker than the ones <u>on</u> the beats (in C "character" departs slightly from the rule). Speak the words before you try to sing them, adapting the tune to the Greek-o-rhythm.

A: My old Man's a dustman; He wears a dust-man's hat....

B: Left foot in, put in your right foot next, and then you shake...

C: For he's a jol-ly splen-did char-ac-ter and so says ev'ry one. And so...

Happy listening, table thumping and enjoy!

Music Recommendations

As many of Tony's music references from his collection are no longer available, he identified a few examples of unusual rhythms for you (in brackets) from these CD's recommended by Trehantiri for their typical Greek rhythms:

Της Γερακίνας Γιός, Ρεμπετικη Τετρας (The Falconer's Son, Rebetika Quartet) Eros 90312 £15.99. Glykeria, Agathonas, Goles & Tsertos sing 15 rebetika songs. *(Track 5, 5-time; Track 8, 4+5-time)*

Ζωντανά στα Εννεα Ογδοα με την Αθηναϊκή Κομπανία (Live at the 9/8 Club with the Athenian Company) Double CD Sony EPC 512320 2 £22.99.

A recent live recording of a Rebetika revivalist group. The 9/8 Club is interestingly named after the 9/8 rhythm of many Rebetika/Zebekiko songs. 43 tracks of Laïka & Rebetika. I prefer these modern recordings in the traditional style to many of the old re-recorded 78s. *(Mostly 2-time or 4-time)*

The Greek : Islands Minos EMI 72435 40259 2 1 £11.99
Traditional Island Music well performed on this compilation CD of 20 tracks. We recognised a few songs from an earlier Yiannis Parios CD and from hearing in Greece, making this a good one for holiday memories. *(Track 15, 7-time)*

Acropolis Now! *by Tony Brown*

It had been many years since old Theo's last visit to Athens and even then only en route to or from his island. But when he landed this time, he'd have a twelve-hour stopover that was going to help him fulfil an ambition that had been gnawing at him all his life. You see, old Theo had always dreamt of standing on the Acropolis overlooking the whole city and watching the sun rise from that ancient ragged hump.

And now he couldn't wait. Gatwick was hot and busy and he groaned out loud when he heard his 22:30 flight was delayed by almost an hour. He'd already been there for five hours. He'd had a meal then wandered through WH Smith staring at unlikely tabloid nonsense and vapid autobiographies, visiting every nook and searching every cranny of the concourse in trying to pass the time. Now, on top of that, he had another hour to kill before take off. There was nothing for it but to find a quiet corner and shut down. Not necessarily to go to sleep but to relax and close his eyes and look forward to his long awaited visit to the city of cities. His Athens.

And so he made himself comfortable. And once he'd stilled his mind and calmed down a little, time passed without much further strain.

By the time Theo stood outside the airport, actually *on* the soil of Greece, it was still dark but growing lighter by the minute. It would be sunrise in about two hours. He felt like a child again, ready to play and although he still had to find his way up to the Acropolis, it was just too good an opportunity to miss and his heart was filled with joy.

But as he strained at the bus stop, biting what was left of his fingernails, he began having second thoughts because every passing second seemed to take forever and already he could see lights being turned off and the sky turning blue-grey before his watery eyes.

And where would he get off the bus once inside the city? What if there was a traffic jam and the time ran out? How would he find the shortest route? Apart from tired, tangled and frazzled nerves draining every bit of self-assurance away, why was he the only one waiting for a bus? Does a bus stop necessarily mean there will be a bus? Would all his romantic notions be dashed beneath the tyres of some nonexistent, ghostly mirage? And where was his friendly backpack? Would it make the journey to Karpathos all alone without his guiding hand? He hadn't set eyes on it since waving it goodbye at check-in and that was hours ago.

So there he stood alone and confused as usual, hands scrunched deep in pockets and pacing circles in the twilight completely marooned. Ah, but at least he was back in Greece and deep down, Theo was incredibly excited with nothing to guide him but his longing.

Then suddenly the bus appeared out of nowhere, shuddering to a halt like some old warhorse, steaming and apologising and gasping for breath as though it had galloped all the way from Troy. It was late but they could just make it as long as there were no more hold ups.

Before he knew it his bus was bouncing through the dark and dusty, multi-laned avenues of Athens, and the very first fingers of a rosy coloured dawn were already scratching through the matted shadows of a brand new day. From his back seat he watched the city stretch and yawn; and in the upper-most windows there was already the hint of a typical golden morning of another sunny day.

Rumbling through the centre where Leoforos Vasilisas Olgas and Amalia meet in one huge open, frantic traffic triangle, exhaust fumes thickened the early purple air as the little bus hissed to a stop at the magnificent Hadrian's Arch.

The stop bears this inscription: *'This is Athens, the ancient city of Theseus.'* Theo smiled. There can't be a more honoured bus stop anywhere on the planet.

The city pavements were crawling with sleepy commuters and it must have been painfully obvious that he was a stranger to the city. That was because he was the only passenger standing in his seat openly gawping at the awe-some Olympian Temple of Zeus looming skyward above the apathetic heads in the crowd. He'd read in school that a jovial cove called Mr. Livy had once remarked, *"Probably the only temple on earth of a size adequate to the greatness of the god."*

So there he sat, dizzy from so much architectural splendour and the on-slaught was almost overwhelming.

A sudden surge of passengers brought Theo to his senses and through the window he caught an electrifying glimpse of something that immediately caused his heart to miss a beat.

Yes, there! Framed in brilliant contrast to the silhouetted buildings of shad-owy Lysikratous Street, he saw the first glowing vision of his goal. The ancient, all knowing, most famous building on earth. Rising above the cramped and bewildering streets of Athens it stood. The Acropolis. Unique and incomparable, and resting upon it, the artistic masterpiece that is The Parthenon.

Theo jumped out of his seat, crushing several toes and chanted his *"signomi"* as he elbowed his way onto the dusty pavement. There was nothing be-tween them now but time and space. The sky had turned grey blue and not a cloud in sight.

And what a day this was already. Breathlessly, Theo paced up the hill, its streets washing away the dirt and dust of the previous day. Up through a

mixture of suave offices and beneath lush eucalyptus. Almost running, he strode past beautiful pastel painted houses, with doors yawning and homely chairs still sitting in the street from last night's gentle conversations.

To Theo, Athens is an unpretentious garden city. It is a city of the people. A mishmash of orderly chaos. And as he grew closer to the summit, he realised a great awareness. Here was he, Theo, on his own personal legs and feet, walking right then, that second, over timeless passages and in the tracks of glorious predecessors, towards the hopelessly joyful Parthenon and all that it means and has meant through two and a half thousand years.

On and up in the fading twilight, he followed the ancient Panathenaic Way until he had to stop for breath. When he did he raised his eyes and felt an amazing rush of gladness. Before him stood the Parthenon, smiling, comforting and encouraging him on. They shared the same air. Its noble face welcomed him that very morning at almost 6:30, that moment, on that day, during his life-span, in that body. There are excited packs of dogs running wild over the Acropolis and it can be disconcerting when you are out of breath and quite alone. But if you walk purposefully and pay silent homage to the god Hermes, the dog-throttler, you will enjoy the protection afforded all wayfarers in that country and your travelling will be safe, even from wild boar, wolves and lions.

With only a few seconds to go, Theo climbed a steep and slippery outcrop on the eastern side of the rocky limestone mass and, with the ancient building on his right, looked in the direction of Immitos Hill, and waited for old Helios to show his face. A small crowd of fans, or sun-worshippers, sat sprinkled over the boulders talking softly. Some had even spent the night there.

Then, in the blink of an eye, there he was. Everyone 'goshed' and 'wowed' as eyelids clicked and flashed. The orange sun took time to show his face from behind the Pendelli Hills, up and high above a polluted haze that was once the pure air of this ancient city-state. Sunbeams strolled through shades of long familiar stone from cream, through cinnamon to honey. Could it really be so soft to touch? Could it be so much like flesh?

Such an emotional spectacle had Theo sitting down in deep respectful silence and allowing the stillness to reclaim him like before.

Down in the city, orange and yellow light began seeping into the cavities and crevices of the labyrinth that is Athens while these gods looked down from their Mount Olympus and marvelled at the wonder that lay before them. On the shiny time-polished cobbles and smooth-worn stoneways just below the gentle temple of Athene Nike, Theo stepped across the centuries and joined her citizens gathering to pay homage to their goddess Pallas Athena in the Great Panathenaia contests. They would consist of processions, festivals and games, and last for six days with several thousand people enthusiastically jumping up and down, paying homage and witnessing all the majesty, pomp and splendour. Someone had told him these contests were only held every four years and always on the anniversary of the Goddess' birthday.

Theo wasn't surprised, it must have been exhausting.

And over on the steps, could that really be Socrates and Plato going on about how great minds had already produced great beauty of every kind *and* celebrated it too? About how easy it was to overlook the political, architectural, artistic, philosophical and ideological significance this monument held for we little humans? About how Greece was the cradle of democracy, medicine, music, art and mathematics? They were deep in conversation.

Theo shook his head in disbelief and began to see that for a wild, flickering second in the rolling calendar of human existence, he'd been in tune with the infinite and even managed to celebrate this awareness in a fizz and a bubble that came to resist the indiscriminate winds of war and fate.

But wait! All this was three thousand years ago!

Theo became restless. This was heavy stuff. He needed to calm down.

Reeling from overload, he wandered through the gates and back to the grey, flat-topped rock where he'd stood at sunrise. And there, beneath the dusty pines and cedars, he lay down on a bench, closed his eyes to the hectic sawing of the cicadas and fell asleep.

A loud female voice woke him with a start.

"Ladies and gentlemen, Flight AMM265D Air2000 London Gatwick to Athens is boarding now. We are sorry for the delay. Will all passengers please make their way to Gate 3 right away."

Pause. *"Ladies and gentlemen, ..."*

Theo yawned and checked his pocket watch. About time too. It was almost midnight. And he was pretty sure he'd been having that dream again...

Advertisers/Supporters - Travel Contacts

When responding to advertisers, please mention that
you saw their name in **Greek-o-File.** We rely on sponsorship from
advertisers as they rely on responses to their adverts.

If you would like to **advertise** in future **Greek-o-File books**,
or send your marketing **'flyers'** on appropriate subjects with our
mailings to direct subscribers, please telephone **01753 544475** or
email **mail@greekofile.co.uk** for information. Rates from just **£35**

ANSWERS

Greek Crossword on page 151

Music Rhythms page 172
A. 5-time,
B. 9-time
C. 7-time

K	A	T	A	Σ	T	H	M	A
A		A		Y				Π
Λ	E	Ξ	I	Λ	O	Γ	I	O
O		I		Λ		E		Δ
K	A	Δ	P	O		M		E
A		I		Γ	I	A	T	I
I	K	A	N	O		T		Ξ
P			A	Σ	K	O	Π	H
I		T	O			Y		
A	N	A	Σ	T	A	Σ	H	Σ

*In this index main article subjects are in **bold**, reference only items in plain text
and place names are listed after their island or region name.*

Greek-o-File™ Company Reg 3620858, VAT Reg GB 711 1751 75

The Greek-o-File Volumes 1 & 2

If you did not read our first 2 volumes, you can still buy them direct from Greek-o-File (or from retail outlets) to build your File on all things Greek. 192 pages, approx 50 illustrated articles in each book.

Volume 1 ISBN 0-9543593-0-5
£8 inc. UK p&p (retail £8.50)

Volume 2 ISBN 0-9543593-1-3
£9 direct (retail £9.50)

or

**OFFER PRICE £15 for
Vol 1 & 2 inc UK P&P.**

<u>Volume 1</u> includes: **Travel Profiles** of Poros, Lefkada, Mykonos Delos & Rinia, Ikaria, plus **many Travel Experiences** & **Guide to UK Tour Operators** 'Who Goes Where in Greece'. **Greek Life** anecdotes, articles and advice inc. Building a dream Home and losing a Greek home to fire, Buying Property in Greece, Getting Married in Greece, Komboloi, Sponges, Wild Flowers and more, **Events** includes Public Holidays 2003 to 2005 and more.

<u>Volume 2</u> includes: **Travel Profiles** of Fourni, Skopelos, Amorgos, Halkidiki, Patmos plus more **Travel Experiences**, **Greek Life** articles include Retiring to Greece, Unemployed in Greece, Athens Street Dogs, Icons, Mining and more.

Plus both books have sections on **Food & Wine, History & Mythology, Language, Events, Book Reviews, Greek Music & Short Story**.

<u>Back Issues</u> of our former **Quarterly Magazines** are also available - published Autumn 1998 to June 2002, A4 prepunched pages build into a file of information and anecdotes. Buy them at **£3 each** (inc UK p&p) or all **15** with a **FREE** white 4 ring Greek-o-**FILE** and dividers for just **£40**. (UK only)

Greek-o-File Logos to personalise your T-shirt, sweatshirt, vest, shorts, sundress, or other cotton item - **Iron-on** Greek-o-File registered trade mark logos **cyan & black** (colour as book front) seagull silhouette & name or just use the seagull **3 logos 6x4cm** for **£1.95** or larger **2 logos 9x6cm** for **£2.50** inc VAT & UK P&P.

Greek-o-File™

Notecards - Images of Greece, Animals, Cats, Flowers, Lesvos or Eresos sets available - 9 cards with envelopes for **£4.20**, **3 sets £11** inc VAT & UK P&P.

Plus additional offers for direct subscribers

Contact Greek-o-File 01753 544475 or mail@greekofile.co.uk for further information, or see website **www.greekofile.co.uk** for more content detail of books, magazine extracts & notecards.

Reply Form

If you would like to be **notified when future issues** are to be published,
order offer items, or send a **contribution for consideration** in future books,
please complete this form (or a copy) where appropriate
and post with relevant additional details or payment to
Greek-o-File, 4 Harvey Road, Langley, Nr Slough, Berks, SL3 8JB, UK, or
contact for more information - Tel **01753 544475**, Email **mail@greekofile.co.uk**.

Name Mr/Mrs/Ms/Miss_____

Address_____

_____

_____Post Code _____

Tel (Day / Eve)_____

Email address _____

Where did you buy/find this book? _____

I would like:

To be notified when future Greek-o-File volumes will be available   ___
If you purchased this book direct you will automatically be notified - let us know if you move.
Circle or underline as appropriate or send separate letter if clarification needed.
Prices quoted **inc UK P&P** on all items and **VAT** on logos and notecards.

To purchase The Greek-o-File Vol 1 & 2   @ **£15** for both   ___

or Individually Vol 1 @ £8, Vol 2 or 3 @ £9   or a set of ALL 3 for **£22**   ___

(For overseas add per book: Rest of EU £1, Rest of World £2)

To purchase ALL 15 Greek-o-File magazine back issues, now offered for **£40** ___
includes UK P&P, a **FREE Greek-o-FILE** (4-ring A4 white file with dividers).
(Individual issues available @ £3 each, telephone for details or see www.greekofile.co.uk)

To purchase Greek-o-File Notecards   1 set of 9 for £4.20,   3 sets £11   ___
- specify sets: Images of Greece, Animals, Cats, Flowers, Lesvos, Eresos

To purchase Greek-o-File logos inc VAT, P&P   2 large (9x6cm) for £2.50 ___
                                                     3 small (6x4cm) for £1.95 ___

I enclose an article/ item for consideration (max 3 x A4 pages, 2,000 words) ___
(Free copy of book supplied to contributors of articles of at least 1 page)

Under the terms of the Data Protection Act we do NOT supply names & addresses to others,
but may send mailings about appropriate products from our offices.

Optional Additional Information:

Favourite Greek destination(s) _____
(max 3)

Age Group   Less than 30 ☐   31-45 ☐   46-60 ☐   61+ ☐

Greek-o-File™ Company Reg. 3620858, VAT Reg GB 711 1751 75